I0201803

Sarah's Spiritual Journey with Jesus

A Channeled Story of Divine Love
& Transformation

Michelle Henderson

Copyright © 2024 by Michelle Henderson.

All right reserved. No part of this publication may be reproduced, distributed, or transmitted in any form or by any means, including photocopying, recording, digital scanning, or other electronic or mechanical methods, without the prior written permission of the publisher, except in the case of brief quotations embodied in critical reviews and certain other noncommercial uses permitted by copyright law. For permission requests, write to the author at the email below.

ISBN Paperback: 979-8-9853253-3-1

Library of Congress Control Number: 2024918898

Printed in the United States of America.

Michelle Henderson
mohenderson2525@gmail.com

Although this publication is designed to provide accurate information in regard to the subject matter covered, the publisher and the author assume no responsibility for errors, inaccuracies, omissions, or any other inconsistencies herein. This publication is meant as a source of valuable information for the reader, however, it is not meant as a replacement for direct expert assistance. If such a level of assistance is required, the services of a competent professional should be sought.

Table Of Contents

A Prelude to Her Story
My Journey to Channeling Sarah

I grew up in a Christian home where Sundays were spent in church with my family. I cherished learning about Jesus and singing hymns with heartfelt conviction. Whenever I felt lonely, frustrated, or confused about life, I would turn to Jesus in prayer. This deep connection made me see Jesus as not just a figure of love and forgiveness, but as a true and trusted friend.

As I grew older, I continued the tradition of attending church, now with my husband and children by my side. Yet, even as I honored this tradition, I always sensed that there was more to spirituality than what I had been taught. Often, when my friends spoke about Jesus, their words didn't resonate with me. I couldn't understand why their perspectives didn't align with the truths that my heart held dear. This led me on a journey of spiritual seeking, as I yearned for knowledge that truly resonated with my soul.

The spiritual world began to reach out to me, and my intuition became heightened. I started to hear spirits communicate with me telepathically, feel the emotions of others, and sense the different energies in various environments. These experiences were new and unfamiliar, and they brought a sense of fear. When I shared my experiences with friends and family, their responses were often laced with fear and warnings of evil. Seeking guidance, I visited my pastor. She encouraged me not to be afraid and reminded me that I was in control. She advised me to speak from the heart and let the spiritual world know if I wasn't ready.

That evening, I communicated with the spiritual world, expressing my need for time to adjust to this new reality. I then sought out a spiritual teacher, a local psychic medium, who guided me through the process of understanding my spiritual gifts.

She taught me that these abilities were not unique to me, but rather gifts that anyone could possess. I began practicing yoga and meditation, using my intuition to support the children and families.

After 30 years of service, I decided it was time to fully embrace and develop my psychic and mediumship abilities.

Four years into my spiritual journey, during a deep meditation, both Jesus and Sarah came to me. Jesus introduced Sarah and asked if she could channel spiritual messages through me—messages the world needed to hear. Instinctively, I knew I had to say yes, even though I didn't know how this would unfold. While I had experience channeling telepathically during mediumship sessions, I had never channeled in a trance state before. I feared losing control and wondered where my soul would go during the process. But I soon realized that these fears were unfounded. Conscious trance channeling allows the person to remain fully aware while another entity speaks through them, using their voice and body. Once I accepted this sacred task, things began to unfold rapidly. I understood that I needed to wear a headpiece during channeling sessions as a symbol of the sacred nature of Sarah's messages. As our energies began to merge, I practiced channeling Sarah's messages for a few close friends, and my trust in her deepened. Several times a week, I recorded videos of Sarah's channelings, where her messages overflowed with love, hope, and divine guidance.

In another meditation, I felt called to channel Sarah's journey with Jesus through automatic writing. As I wrote, vivid images accompanied each word, allowing me to experience what Sarah felt during those profound events. Her unconditional love for Jesus, for those she knew, and for the world was palpable. She played a significant role in Jesus' spiritual mission. Some of the events she recounts may challenge your current beliefs, but isn't that the essence of being a spiritual seeker? We are guided by our curiosity to uncover deeper spiritual wisdom.

Today, many are searching for their own spiritual truth as the energy of our world is shifting, awakening people to their spiritual path. I hope that Sarah's story brings you new awareness, truth, wisdom, and above all, love.

Michelle

Section 1:
Sarah's Spiritual Journey
With Jesus

Chapter 1

My First Encounter with Jesus

I Sarah, walked among Jesus. I lived in a small village with my father, a sweet and thoughtful man who raised me after my mother died from childbirth complications. It was not an easy task for him in those times, but he protected me and made me feel safe. Every evening after a long, hard day, I prepared meals for us, mostly bread, and felt grateful despite our simple fare. When he passed, his face lit up with a peaceful readiness to reunite with my mother. I buried him next to our house, finding myself alone but not afraid, for my father had taught me to embrace life.

Knowing I needed a trade to survive, I turned to pottery. I had nothing to offer a man to take care of me, so I had to fend for myself. At the market, I kept my gaze down, blending in with the crowd. Pottery was integral to daily life—people drank from pottery cups and ate from pottery plates. Living near a clay-rich area, I would pray with gratitude each time I gathered clay from the earth. My feet were perpetually discolored from the clay, a testament to my work.

I learned the craft by watching townswomen and was especially drawn to making wine pitchers, items that brought joy to people. It took months before I had enough pieces to sell, and I enjoyed decorating them with triangle designs. My friend Mary often kept me company while I worked and helped me take my pottery to market.

The day I met Jesus was a glorious one. I woke early, greeted by the warmth and peace of the sunrise. It was another day of selling pottery, and I loaded my cart with Mary's help before she had to tend to her mother. As I sat with my wares, I felt a presence. Hesitant to look up, fearing unwanted attention, I heard a soft voice ask why I made pottery. Feeling safe, my gaze moved from his feet to his smiling, glowing face. It was Jesus. Speaking very softly, he asked me why I did my pottery. Finding my voice, I explained that I made pottery to sell, but Jesus shook his head gently.

"No," he said, "Why do you make pottery?"

I told him I enjoyed turning a handful of clay into something useful and beautiful, something that connected people to the earth. Jesus smiled, his presence comforting like my father's. He asked my name and inquired about the triangle designs. I explained that I felt compelled to add them to complete my creations.

Jesus then mentioned a gathering a mile out of town at a campsite, where people would come together to make plans or simply talk. It was a familiar place where Mary and I often met our friends. He invited me to join them at sundown, and I asked if I could bring Mary along.

"Yes, bring whoever you want to," he said.

I asked him what his favorite piece of pottery was. He told me it was the smallest pitcher.

"It might be small, but it's meant for big things."

Knowing that Jesus traveled often and likely had no need for pottery, I asked if he wanted to take it anyway. He appreciated the gesture but said he couldn't carry it everywhere. Instead, he told me to bring it to the camp along with my favorite drink. I watched him walk away, eager to share the news with Mary. After Jesus left, I could hardly wait to see him again. His smile was safe and loving.

I managed to sell a piece to a woman who admired its craftsmanship and wanted to use it at her family's dinner table. With the money, I bought wine for the pitcher Jesus wanted me to bring. There was no time to go home; I was too excited. When Mary came by to help with my pottery, she was thrilled to hear about my encounter with Jesus. She had heard about him from others in the city. We loaded my pottery onto the cart, stopped to buy more wine and some fruit for supper, and felt like children embarking on an adventure.

Reflections of Chapter 1

1. How do you think Sarah's relationship with her father shaped her character and her ability to face challenges after his death?

2. The craft of pottery is central to this chapter. What do you think the pottery symbolizes in Sarah's life, and how does it connect to her spiritual journey?

3. Sarah describes feeling a sense of comfort and familiarity when meeting Jesus. What do you think it was about Jesus that evoked these feelings, and how does this reflect the idea of divine presence in everyday life?

4. Why do you think Jesus asked Sarah why she made pottery, and how do you interpret her response about connecting people to the earth?

5. The triangle designs on Sarah's pottery seem significant to her. What might these designs represent, and how do they tie into the themes of the chapter?

6. Sarah was hesitant to make eye contact at the market but felt safe looking at Jesus. What does this reveal about her internal state and her perception of others?

7. Consider Sarah's decision to follow Jesus' invitation to the gathering. What does this decision signify about her faith, curiosity, or need for connection?

8. How does the interaction between Sarah and Jesus reflect the broader themes of simplicity, humility, and purpose in life?

9. What do you think is the significance of Jesus choosing the smallest pitcher and his comment about it being "meant for big things"? How might this foreshadow future events in Sarah's life?

10. If you were in Sarah's position, how would you have responded to Jesus' questions and invitation? What does this tell you about your own values and beliefs?

Chapter 2:

The Camp of Jesus

In the Presence of Miracles

A s we approached the camp, a man named Matthew greeted us and helped move the cart. He was friendly and showed us where to sit. Jesus came over to welcome us, and I handed him the wine. He bowed and thanked us for our generosity. We waited a few minutes as Jesus ensured everyone who wanted to be there had arrived. I recognized several women from the market. A fire burned near where Jesus stood, and everyone sat in silence, anticipating his words.

Jesus welcomed everyone and asked us to hold hands, calling us his brothers and sisters. He led us in a prayer of love and peace, asking us to repeat certain phrases aloud. The atmosphere grew charged with energy. Jesus explained that by coming together as one, our collective soul power strengthened. Afterward, he invited us to meditate, clearing our minds to allow the Holy Spirit to enter.

I found it difficult to clear my mind, still buzzing with excitement. Others began to speak in a heavenly language I had never heard. Unable to focus, I opened my eyes and witnessed a miracle: a glowing light surrounded Jesus, connecting to each of us. My hands glowed too.

Jesus opened his eyes and said, "May the gift of light forever shine in love."

Everyone then opened their eyes. Overwhelmed and enlightened, I fell to my knees. Mary was the first to ask if I was okay, and I heard myself sobbing. Suddenly, Jesus appeared before me.

"My sister, please stand," he said. Summoning all my strength, I stood. Jesus placed his hand over my heart and said, "May you learn what your heart, your soul is trying to tell you. May you embrace and love who you truly are."

I felt so much peace and energy flowing through me that I could not speak.

Jesus gazed at everyone. "Does anyone want to share what they received from the heavens?"

Only silence filled the air until my friend Mary spoke up. "May I share?" she asked.

"Yes, sister, please share," Jesus replied.

There was a gasp from a man in the crowd. Jesus addressed him before Mary could continue. "Do you have something to say?" he asked.

The man responded, "Women are not supposed to speak at meetings attended by men."

With love in his voice, Jesus said, "In the eyes of heaven, do you think God made only men in his image? He also made women in his image as well. Men and women will receive messages from the heavens since they are of God's essence."

Mary began to speak. "I saw many angels of light showing me that they are always around us to love and protect us. They protect us from dangerous situations that occur on earth. They wanted us to know that we can call on them when we need them."

Jesus thanked her for sharing her message. He told us that our messages are sacred to us and us alone, meant to help guide us in the present. He then asked if anyone else wanted to share, but no one else spoke up. I, Sarah, had to deeply reflect on what had been given to me.

Jesus told us that if we wanted to come again the next night, the camp would be east of Jordan, following the earth's directions.

Our meeting would raise the vibrational energy of the town.

"For now, let us drink and eat to worship our time together. Be grateful for your blessings," he said. With those words, everyone yelled and smiled, celebrating our soul gathering.

I took my wine pitcher from Jesus and served others. Mary and I sat together. As we ate, I told her how proud I was of her for sharing her sacred message. She told me she felt a calling to share and believed it was important for everyone to do so. Jesus came over to us and asked if we were coming tomorrow.

Mary replied, "As long as Sarah is coming."

I laughed and reassured them I would be there. Jesus sat down and asked us about our families. Mary came from a traditional family and expressed her fear that they might not approve of her attending the camp meetings. Jesus told her to speak the truth lovingly and offered to speak to them on her behalf. Then, Jesus turned his attention to me. I explained that I was alone, my father having died a few years ago, and that Mary and her mother helped provide food for me.

Jesus replied that the Lord was good and provided what we needed, but we had to ask. He told us that Matthew and Thomas would help us with the cart and walk us home. He acknowledged that while God made us equals, our earthly brothers often did not see it that way.

Reflections on Chapter 2

1. How does the gathering around the fire with Jesus reflect the themes of unity and collective spiritual strength? What do you think is the significance of everyone holding hands and sharing in the prayer?

2. Sarah struggles to clear her mind during the meditation but then witnesses a miraculous light. How does this experience contribute to her spiritual growth and understanding?

3. The chapter highlights a moment of gender tension when a man questions Mary's right to speak. How does Jesus' response to this challenge reveal his views on gender equality? How does this interaction shape your understanding of the roles of women in spiritual communities?

4. Mary shares a vision of angels protecting humanity. How does this vision relate to the broader themes of divine guidance and protection in the memoir?

5. When Jesus places his hand over Sarah's heart and speaks to her about embracing who she truly is, it becomes a pivotal moment for her. What do you think this moment signifies for Sarah's personal journey and future decisions?

6. Jesus emphasizes that the messages received from the heavens are sacred and personal. Why do you think he encourages the sharing of these messages in a communal setting? What might be the purpose of this shared spiritual experience?

7. Consider the symbolic significance of the glowing light that connects Jesus to everyone at the gathering. How does this imagery contribute to the chapter's message about the interconnectedness of all beings?

8. Sarah and Mary both express concerns about how others might perceive their participation in these gatherings. How does this reflect the social and cultural challenges they face? What do these challenges say about the broader societal context in which the story is set?

9. The chapter ends with a sense of community and celebration. How does this closing scene reinforce the themes of gratitude and togetherness that are woven throughout the chapter?

10. Jesus reassures Sarah and Mary that God provides what they need but emphasizes the importance of asking. How does this idea of asking for divine help resonate with you? How might this principle apply to your own life?

Chapter 3:

A Night of Shadow & Light

M y heart sank as Mary and I left the camp, with Thomas kindly helping me with my cart. There was a sense of comfort in knowing we had our own protection. My house was our first stop, and we walked in silence, each of us reflecting on the events at the campfire. When we arrived, I asked Thomas to place the cart beneath a large tree, where it would be safely hidden. I then embraced Mary and bid both Matthew and Thomas farewell, wishing them well as they continued on their way.

We lived outside of Jerusalem. My father sought privacy after my mother's passing. I provided him company and helped with daily chores. After his death, I stayed in the shelter for the same reason: privacy. As a female living alone, it was considered lowly and dangerous. No one would want to marry me as I had nothing to offer —no money or nice items.

When Thomas, Matthew, and Mary left, my heart felt alone. I made sure the opening to my house was blocked and secured. I lit a candle and poured myself some wine. Then I heard a noise outside. I suddenly did not feel alone. It was like the wind blew something in.

The noise grew louder, and I realized I had an intruder. Quickly, I blew out the candle and could still smell the smoke. The intruder entered my house. He was large, but it was too dark to see him clearly. He found me and slapped me across the face. I felt the burning on my cheek and tasted blood. I couldn't speak.

He yelled, "So you think you and your friend can speak in public like men? I will treat you like the woman you are."

He must have followed us to the house. Paralyzed by fear and his strength, I couldn't move. He violated me. As he did, I began to see light in my head.

I saw my father, who told me everything would be okay. I could feel his love. As my body lost awareness, a light surrounded me, and I saw a beautiful woman approaching with a radiant smile. She didn't speak, but I could hear her. She told me I had a beautiful, loving spirit and much to show the world. She also said the heavens were always with me. I knew this angelic being was my mother, whom I had never known. I felt her loving energy leaving and reached out to her.

"Go in love."

I couldn't hold back my tears. I felt someone holding my hand as I opened my eyes. Jesus and Mary were looking down at me.

"There she is. Sarah, you are safe. Try to breathe and relax," Jesus said.

I could smell the oils they had placed on my body. Jesus' hand was on my head, and I felt peaceful energy radiating through me. After a few minutes, Jesus asked me to sit up. I felt as if I had slept for two full moons. As I sat up, I saw my younger self standing next to Mary. Younger Sarah smiled at me and then disappeared.

Mary looked very concerned. Jesus reassured me that all was well and gave Mary and me privacy. I assured her I was okay. Mary kept holding my hand. I suddenly realized I was lying in my cart, which was made up as a bed with a blanket over me. Mary told me she came to my house to help me get ready for the market. When she approached the opening, she knew something was wrong. Everything I owned was scattered everywhere. She found me on the bed in a pool of blood. My hair and face were so covered in blood that she thought I was dead.

She ran back to Jesus' camp.

Jesus and some followers came to my house. When Jesus saw me, he told Mary to get water to clean me up. As she returned, Jesus held her and told her I would be okay. Mary bathed me while others prepared the cart to take me back to camp. Mary said it took over an hour to clean me. She found clean clothes and redressed me, her tears helping to wash away the blood. Once she was done, she told everyone I was clean.

Jesus instructed them to carry me carefully to the cart and get a blanket. He told Mary to gather anything important from my house since I would not be returning. Jesus returned with a cup.

"Here, please drink these herbs. They should make you rest and feel better."

I drank it, feeling my eyes grow heavy. The last thing I remembered was Jesus telling me I was safe.

Reflections for Chapter 3

1. How does the contrast between the darkness of the intruder's actions and the light of the visions Sarah experiences highlight the spiritual battle between fear and love?

2. Sarah's visions of her father and mother provide comfort during her trauma. How do these visions reflect the presence of divine love and guidance in times of deep suffering?

3. Jesus and Mary's roles in Sarah's recovery emphasize their compassion and healing presence. How does this scene reflect the concept of spiritual healing and the role of community in the healing process?

4. The appearance of Sarah's younger self during her recovery suggests a reconnection with her innocence and purity. What might this signify in terms of her spiritual journey and the restoration of her soul?

5. Sarah's encounter with an angelic vision of her mother offers her reassurance and love. How does this encounter with a divine being shape Sarah's understanding of her own spiritual essence and purpose?

6. The intruder's attack is a stark reminder of the dangers Sarah faces as a woman living alone. How does her experience reflect the spiritual challenges of vulnerability and the need for divine protection?

7. After the trauma, Sarah is surrounded by the loving care of Jesus, Mary, and their followers. How does this scene illustrate the power of spiritual community in providing safety and comfort?

8. The chapter ends with Jesus giving Sarah a drink of herbal medicine to help her rest. How does this simple act symbolize the integration of physical and spiritual healing?

9 Sarah's house, once a place of privacy and safety, becomes a site of violence. How does her departure from this home signify a shift in her spiritual path and her readiness to embrace a new chapter in her life?

10. What role does forgiveness play in this chapter, both for Sarah and for the reader's understanding of the spiritual teachings within the memoir?

Chapter 4:

A New Beginning

M ary told me I had slept for hours, never leaving my side. As I slowly awoke, I could hear others talking nearby. Gently, Mary asked if I could sit up and handed me a plate of food and some wine. With each bite, I felt my strength returning, though I still couldn't quite comprehend what had happened. Suddenly, a wave of emotion overcame me, and I began to sob. Mary held me close as Jesus approached. Softly, he asked if he could take my hand. I hesitated and told him I was now unclean, but he simply shook his head.

He reached out and said, "You radiate love and energy, and this type of energy is glorious and always clean. Your soul is always clean. Please take my hand."

I gripped his hand and felt peaceful energy flow through me. Then I heard him pray. "May you always have peace and love. You have empowerment. Don't let another soul take this empowerment from you. Find forgiveness and love. Call the angels, God, and the heavens to you. When you cry, we all cry. May you be blessed."

I thanked him and sat quietly for a few minutes before asking Mary to help me out of the cart so I could stand. I didn't want to miss the campfire festivities, and I needed to ask Jesus what he meant when he said I wouldn't return home. Mary and I found a spot under a tree, where we watched as others began to arrive. I could feel eyes on me.

Mary gently pointed out that my face still bore the marks of battle; it was swollen. She took my hand, and in that moment, I felt both safe and deeply grateful for her unwavering devotion. We sat in peaceful silence, simply enjoying the moment.

The night was a miracle. More women were present. Jesus asked everyone to find a comfortable place. I heard the fire crackling and smelled the burning bark. Jesus raised his arms high to welcome us, calling us brothers and sisters. My heart jumped when I heard my name.

Jesus asked, "Sarah, can you come join me?"

Finding strength in my legs, I walked over to him. He gently asked if I would hold his hand, and I nodded, placing my hand in his.

Jesus then looked at everyone gathered and said, "We need to pray to the heavens for Sister Sarah."

Everyone joined hands around the fire. As Jesus prayed, a powerful energy surged through me, making me feel lightheaded. Voices began to rise, speaking in different languages. I listened intently for my own light language. Then, unexpectedly, I started singing unfamiliar notes. How could this be? Tears welled up in my eyes. After a few moments, Jesus asked everyone to sit. He told us he was ready to channel a heavenly message.

"Brothers and sisters, I want you to know that, yes, good things happen to good people, but also bad things can happen to good people. Sister Sarah experienced a violent event, even though we don't know why. We must have faith that we are protected by angels and warriors from the spiritual world. What happened to Sarah happened to us. We are Sarah, and Sarah is us. What she feels, we feel. Unfortunately, our society does not practice this. There are many rules that do not seem fair, but these are the times we live in. Many will think Sarah is not clean. This is judgment. Sarah shines bright in her soul. All of our bodies are not as clean as our souls. We should not cast this negative thinking onto Sarah. What happened to Sarah is unjust. She will grieve, as we will grieve with her. Lessons are learned through our emotions. Forgiveness will be at the forefront of the emotions. We do not know anything about Sarah's attacker, but he is part of us. This is a new beginning for Sarah, her friend Mary cleansed her. With each new wipe with a cloth, new pathways to Sarah's journey were opened. Angels sang as Mary completed this ritual. The heavens were open for a short amount of time. Sarah has much to do in her lifetime. Let's honor and love Sarah. Let's not let this event define her. The black cloud over her is changed to an abundance of light. Sarah is not able to go back to her home. Our society is dangerous. Sarah, we want to invite you to walk with us. We want to spread this light energy and messages from the heavens. We welcome you with open arms. Women need to hear your words. Your words will be channeled from the heavens. Women need hope. Women need faith. They need to hear from another woman. Sarah, will you take on this new role in your life?"

I gazed at Mary. She was crying but also smiling.

"Yes, Jesus. I will walk with you and your followers. I accept my new life. I will always follow the light. I forgive not only the man who came into my home last evening but anyone in my life who has had ill will towards me." I felt loving energy piercing my body.

Jesus hugged me and said, "With our sister healing and our accepting her new life, let's celebrate!"

Everyone clapped and yelled. More wine and food were brought in for the evening, which I will never forget. A new life, a new beginning. The fire had to be fed several times during the celebration. Jesus ended the celebration with a prayer and a blessing.

Reflections on Chapter 4

1. How does the act of Jesus holding Sarah's hand, despite her feeling "unclean," reflect the deeper spiritual truth about the purity of the soul versus the body?

2. Jesus speaks of the importance of forgiveness in Sarah's healing process. How does the concept of forgiveness play a role in spiritual growth and transformation, especially in the context of trauma?

3. The chapter highlights the idea that "what happened to Sarah happened to us." How does this concept of shared experience and collective empathy align with spiritual teachings on unity and interconnectedness?

4. Sarah's acceptance of her new role as a messenger and healer is a pivotal moment. How does this transition signify a deeper spiritual calling, and what lessons can we draw about the nature of spiritual vocations?

5. The transformation of the "black cloud" over Sarah into an "abundance of light" is a powerful metaphor. What does this imagery suggest about the process of healing and the potential for spiritual renewal after suffering?

6. How does Mary's role in cleansing Sarah and supporting her through this ordeal exemplify the power of spiritual sisterhood and community in the healing process?

7. Jesus emphasizes that bad things can happen to good people. How does this acknowledgment of suffering within a spiritual context help us reconcile the presence of pain and injustice in the world?

8. Sarah's decision to forgive her attacker and those who have wronged her is a profound act of faith. What does this teach us about the spiritual power of forgiveness, and how can this be applied in our own lives?

9. The celebration at the end of the chapter marks a new beginning for Sarah. How does this communal act of joy and gratitude reinforce the themes of rebirth and renewal in the spiritual journey?

10. In accepting her new life and role, Sarah commits to spreading light and hope to other women. What does this commitment say about the responsibility of those who have experienced spiritual awakenings to guide and support others?

Chapter 5:

Spiritual Lessons in the Camp

E veryone stood in line to say their goodbyes to Jesus. I said my goodbyes to sweet Mary. She wanted to stay, but her family would not allow it. I sat under the tree, contemplating the day's events. I had so many questions, but I was not afraid. The men who stayed with Jesus had gone to ensure that every woman made it safely home.

Jesus was talking to an older woman. He walked over to me with her. I stood up to greet her.

"Sarah, this is Shaloma. She will be staying with us until we move further from town. I want you to feel comfortable with my family. My family are people who stay with my brothers and now you, my sister."

"Thank you, Jesus. I have so many questions," I said, my voice filled with curiosity.

He grinned warmly and nodded. "I know you do. Let's talk while we wait for our brothers to return."

He refilled our wine glasses.

"Jesus, when did you know that you were meant to spread the word of the heavens to everyone? I've also heard you can heal."

My heart began to race as I awaited his response. Jesus got quiet for a moment.

"My mother always knew I had a spiritual mission, but she wanted me to enjoy a normal childhood. Like any child, I was curious about the world around me. I had a spiritual friend who was always by my side—a comforting presence with light hair who appeared whenever I needed her. My brothers grew jealous when they realized I had a spiritual calling, but we remained close. Some of my best memories are of us wrestling and play-fighting with sticks. My father believed it was important to learn a trade, so my brothers and I often practiced building things for the house. My brother Thomas was much better at it than I was. I once made a baby bed, only to discover it was too wobbly to use. We all had a good laugh over it. It was all in good fun.

My childhood was largely uneventful, just as my parents intended. They knew that my spiritual journey would be extraordinary, so they felt a quiet, sheltered life was what I needed. They protected me, fearing I might leave home too soon. I practiced the Jewish faith with my family and was held accountable for my mistakes, like any child. I vividly remember the time I was caught in a lie—it never happened again after that. My father had a whip, and though it stung, it seemed to pain him just as much as it did me.

As my brothers found companionship, I began to feel lonely. My mother, always supportive, understood that everyone needs someone. One day, she introduced me to a local woman named Sahara. She was beautiful, with a gracious heart, and we talked for hours. It felt as though our energies were deeply connected. Later, as I sat in meditation, I wondered if I should pursue this relationship, knowing my spiritual calling was ahead. I prayed to the heavens for guidance, and the message I kept hearing was, 'Follow your heart.'

When I spoke to my mother about it, she assured me that I deserved the happiness and joy that love could bring. Sahara understood my spiritual path and promised to support me. She told me that when the angels called me to change the world, she would let me go without hesitation. My parents welcomed her and told me that Sahara would live with them.

Our wedding ceremony was rooted in Jewish tradition. Sahara glowed with happiness, and I knew we had many joyful memories ahead of us. As a special gift, my mother gave us small wooden statues of ourselves, beautifully crafted with her precise wood-carving skills. Sahara and I cherished these pieces deeply."

We began to hear the other brothers coming back to camp. Jesus stopped and told Shaloma and me to get some rest.

As I lay on my bed, gazing up at the stars, I couldn't help but feel they each had a story to tell. The same sky had watched over those who came before us, connecting us across time. I wondered what my story would be. What would the stars say about me after I was gone?

The next morning, after a plate full of fruit and twigs, I began to feel more like myself again. The bruises on my face had faded, but I still felt the deeper battle scars. I knew it would take time to fully heal. My thoughts wandered to the stranger who had attacked me, and I wondered why he carried so much anger. God gave us emotions to experience life, but what if those emotions hurt mankind? I may never understand why he felt the need to harm me. I also wondered if people were angry with Jesus because he embodied love. Just as I was lost in thought, Paul interrupted me.

"Sarah, do you want to go to town with me to let others know that we will be moving west of town?"

My heart yearned to be with others and to have a purpose. "Yes, I'll go. Thank you."

Paul and I left while the others prepared to move everything west of town. He was kind and respectful, but quiet and often kept to himself. I had to ask him questions just to learn more about him. This curiosity of mine often got me into trouble as a woman, especially in a time when we were expected to serve men and make as little eye contact as possible. But I couldn't help my fascination with the world and the people in it. My father always indulged my questions, no matter how silly they seemed, and he honored my curiosity.

So, naturally, I asked Paul many questions. He told me about his rough childhood, how his father was strict and demanding with rigid rules that Paul could never seem to live up to. Despite his best efforts, he never felt like he could please his father, but he learned early on how to be tough. Paul also shared that he had been forced into a marriage without love, a relationship built more on survival than affection. But when he met Jesus, he felt a new calling in life. Before leaving his family, he made sure they were taken care of.

As harsh as our society could be, people relied on their support systems not just for comfort, but for survival. Trust was essential—without it, your very life could be at risk. Thankfully, the market was filled with familiar faces, people I knew and trusted.

Paul encouraged me to reach out to the women I knew, inviting more of them to join us around the campfire. I spoke to many, but some were too afraid to come. Paul told several of them that I would be speaking from the heavens that night. Hearing this made me nervous, but I placed my trust in Jesus and the supportive community gathered around the campfire.

Paul looked at me and said it was time for a break. He found a spot in a beautiful garden and promised to return with food. As I sat there, I felt an overwhelming sense of peace, surrounded by the vibrant life all around me. When Paul returned, I was eager to talk and ask questions, but after he blessed the food, he gently told me we needed to sit in silence.

Smiling, he explained that sitting in peace would help him receive messages from heaven. The food felt sacred, and it was a comfort to share a moment of quiet with someone, unburdened by words.

When we returned, everyone was meditating in silence, their faces radiating peace. Paul gestured for me to sit and join them in meditation. I closed my eyes, but my mind was restless, filled with constant thoughts. Suddenly, I sensed someone beside me.

When I opened my eyes, I saw it was Jesus. He had sat down next to me and gently instructed me to breathe with him. He counted as we took deep breaths, even holding them for a moment.

Gradually, I felt my body begin to relax. Jesus placed his hand over my heart and told me to breathe into it, explaining that the heart is a messenger with much to say, but I needed to clear my mind to truly hear it. He continued to sit by my side, and I think it was the most blissful state I have ever experienced. Tears welled up in my eyes, and Jesus tenderly held my hand.

After a few moments, Jesus announced that it was time to move on to the next camp. I still had my cart, which we filled with supplies. As we walked, I found myself alongside Shaloma, unable to keep pace with the men. Curious, I asked Shaloma where she was from. She shared that she lived in a small town east of the mountains, where she had cared for her mother and father. Though she never married—a situation often seen as a disgrace—she remained devoted to her parents until she met Jesus. Shaloma knew in her heart that she wanted to follow Jesus as he spread the good news to everyone. Her parents supported her decision, though her younger sister, who saw Shaloma as a mother figure, was reluctant to let her go. They invited Jesus to dinner and enjoyed his visit.

During the meal, he asked her parents for their blessing, explaining that he needed women to be part of his camp festivities, emphasizing the importance of having women present at the gatherings. Her parents were thrilled that Shaloma would be part of something so meaningful.

As we walked, my feet began to ache, and Shaloma kindly offered to heat water and massage my feet when we reached the camp. Grateful, I held her hand and felt truly blessed.

Once we arrived at the new camp, we set down all the supplies and began setting up, just as we had at the previous camp, including the fire. Shaloma got a bucket full of water and told me to sit near the fire. After cleansing the water, we drank it. Then, Shaloma poured some of the water into a large bowl and gently placed my feet into it. The sensation was pure bliss. She closed her eyes and began to pray, her words soon shifting into a different language.

As she massaged my feet, I felt a surge of energy course through my leg. I closed my eyes, absorbing the experience.

The next thing I knew, I woke up wrapped in blankets. As I looked around, I noticed new people had arrived at the camp, including an older gentleman being carried by his sons. Jesus encouraged his brothers and sisters to nourish their bodies, and everyone began eating the sweet berries. I sat down beside Shaloma to thank her. Jesus then stood in front of the fire, welcoming everyone and inviting them to gather close. He asked us all to join together as one in prayer.

"Thank you for the fresh air that we breathe, the water that replenishes, the ground that allows us to rest, and the fire that brings our bodies warmth. Please allow me to speak the divine truth as it always has been. Now everyone, please find your spiritual voice."

Everyone began speaking the heavenly languages. It was a beautiful song with different instruments playing one song. After a few minutes, Jesus asked for the elder gentleman to be placed in the front. His son laid him down on my blankets. Jesus said, "Brothers and sisters, we have a brother who needs healing. My healing alone can heal him, but everyone's energy together is so much more spiritual. Let's come together. Place a hand down on the brother as you continue with your heavenly language."

I placed my hand on his shoulder. The man began to shake. He began to groan and growl. Everyone kept speaking their language.

Once the man settled down, Jesus said, "May you be healed with love and light. May you release all the burdens you have. Do you accept our love and healing?"

The man was crying and said, "Yes, I do."

Jesus said, "Now, rest."

As the man rested, Jesus asked if anyone would want to speak a message. He asked if a sister would want to speak. I was grateful, so I told Jesus that I wanted to speak. With my legs shaking, I asked the heavens to speak through me.

"When I first met my brothers and sisters, I was alone and felt that most people did not want to spend time with me. My only friend, Mary, was always there for me. She was an angel. My brothers and sisters were strangers, but showed unconditional love. I have learned that I deserve this love because I am a part of everyone. We are all one. I know my truth and my purpose now. I want to help Jesus spread the heavenly messages for our people to hear. I feel safe. I'm a woman and this could be dangerous, but with the divine's love, I'm willing to take a chance. My brothers and sisters, let's help Jesus connect with the people who need to know the heavenly truths."

Jesus came over to thank me. He looked around to everyone and stated, "As Sarah said, let's plant our seeds and witness our garden grow."

As the fire got lower, people began to leave. Many of our brothers left to help others get home safely. I had so many questions for Jesus and hoped we would have a chance to talk. I waited by the fire until Jesus was alone. He actually walked towards me.

"Do you have any questions for me?"

I could feel my jaw drop. "Yes. How did you know?"

He laughed and told me that he is told things that are important. He sat next to me. I asked him where his wife was. Jesus smiled at this question.

"My wife, Sahara, is living with her family, and our children are growing up so quickly. Yes, my family is doing well. I asked a brother to send them messages on my behalf, ensuring they are in a safe place. My spiritual quest will be dangerous, and I want to make sure they are protected. Sahara always knew I would have to leave, just as many of our brothers have left their families behind. We are meant to have human experiences, and I was meant to grow up in a Jewish home, to live a normal childhood, and to have a family of my own so I could relate to others on this mission. It's never easy to leave your family, but knowing they are safe is a true gift. As the time for my departure drew closer, the angels began visiting me more often. To prepare for my journey, I found myself meditating more frequently, which led to a deep spiritual awakening. I started having visions of what was destined to come. I felt both honored and grateful to know I would help bring about change in the name of love. The angels revealed that I would channel messages from the heavens and possess healing and magical abilities. These abilities are available to all humans, but they must choose to embrace them. Many of our ancestors once understood how to harness these gifts, but over time, learning and knowledge began to overshadow their importance. Our ancestors wanted humans to be in charge of their abilities. This would happen over time. Learning will take place with each generation. The children will not only learn from their parents, but they will change things for progress. Each new tool will be channeled through its maker.Sarah, you have to witness my teachings and the events that occur. Most of my followers are men. We need the eyes of a woman to witness these events as well. Try to write as much as you can. Other sisters who are with us are doing the same. For now, get some rest. It's going to be another busy day."

Reflections on Chapter 5

1. How does Jesus' conversation with Sarah about his childhood and spiritual mission provide insight into his human experience and divine calling? What does this reveal about the balance between living a normal life and fulfilling a spiritual destiny?

2. Sarah's growing sense of purpose and her acceptance of her new role is a significant moment in this chapter. How does this transition reflect the idea of divine calling and the responsibilities that come with spiritual awakening?

3. The chapter highlights the importance of silence and meditation, particularly in the scenes with Paul and later with Jesus. How does the practice of silence contribute to spiritual growth and the ability to receive divine guidance?

4. Jesus speaks about the need for both men and women to witness and document his teachings. How does this reflect the importance of diverse perspectives in spiritual journeys and the role of women in spiritual communities?

5. The scene where Jesus heals the elderly man with the help of the entire community emphasizes the power of collective spiritual energy. How does this communal approach to healing reflect the broader spiritual principle of interconnectedness?

6. Sarah's speech about feeling safe and accepted within the community despite the dangers she faces as a woman is a powerful moment. How does this experience illustrate the role of faith and community in overcoming fear and societal limitations?

7. In this chapter, Sarah wonders about the motivations behind the actions of her attacker and the emotions that harm mankind. How does this reflection on human emotions and their impact on others contribute to the chapter's spiritual themes?

8. Jesus shares with Sarah the importance of her role in witnessing and recording his teachings, particularly as a woman. How does this task of witnessing and documentation serve as a spiritual responsibility, and what lessons can be drawn from it for our own lives?

9. The imagery of planting seeds and witnessing the garden grow is used by Jesus to describe the spreading of spiritual teachings. How does this metaphor resonate with the chapter's themes of growth, transformation, and the spread of divine truth?

10. Jesus' conversation with Sarah about his family and the sacrifices made for his spiritual quest highlights the challenges of balancing human relationships with divine missions. How does this discussion deepen your understanding of the personal sacrifices involved in spiritual leadership?

Chapter 6:

A Divine Transformation

H e was right! The next day, many people from the town came to visit. Word had spread about the healing that took place the night before. Jesus asked everyone to sit down so that he could begin another gathering. He invited everyone to hold hands as they started, but since there were so many newcomers, he did not ask us to speak in our heavenly language.

As we held hands, Jesus asked everyone to come with open, loving hearts. The heavens were open, and Jesus, along with his followers, was ready to share messages and perform healings. He then began to sing, and as the new people relaxed, smiles began to spread across their faces. After his song, we were asked to sit comfortably. Here was Jesus, teaching his brothers and sisters.

"We come together to witness the power and wisdom that God has for us. We need to make sure that we listen and learn what we need to with the time spent. Do you have love in your home? A home without love is a dark place where a candlelight cannot be seen. It is difficult to keep love in the home when our earthly tasks and problems keep the darkness not only in our homes, but in our hearts. Find the gratitude for what you have. If you only have a rock to sleep on, be thankful for the rock. If you live with someone who is abusive to you, try to find gratitude for being alive. Pray to the heavens to make things better. When you talk to the heavens, you are also talking to your soul. Open your heart to possibilities. Can God not change your life? You are loved. You are special. You need to look for miracles here. When babies are born, that's a miracle. When flowers bloom, that's a miracle. Each time you take a breath, that is a miracle. I want you to pray for what you need and then be grateful and thank the heavens for the good things in your life. Remember, you are part of the plan. Let's pray."

After we prayed, Jesus asked all of his followers to stand next to him so that we could heal. The first person who wanted healing was a young girl. Her parents told us that she was always tired and always looked pale. We put our hands on her. Jesus began to pray and then told us to use our heavenly language. I could feel energy pulsing through my hands.

A bright light appeared in my mind, and I found myself needing to breathe more deeply. Suddenly, the young girl began to shake, startling me at first, but I could hear Jesus continuing his prayer. Then, without warning, a cold wind seemed to sweep through, and the girl began to throw up. Jesus's voice grew louder, and then, just as suddenly, the girl became still. Jesus gently instructed her to rest, and we released our hands from her. He then turned to look at her parents.

"Give her more water and nutritious fruit for the next few days. She had some blackness in her intestines."

The parents kissed his hand in gratitude.

We continued healing through the night, working for several hours and helping five people. By the end of the night, we were exhausted. After everyone had left, Jesus explained that we had used a great deal of energy to heal others, which is why we felt so tired. However, he reassured us that there is an abundance of energy; the heavens are made of energy, and so are we. He compared it to the sun's rays hitting our bodies—when we feel tired, it's a sign that a lot of energy has passed through us.

He explained that while he could heal on his own, he wants to show others that they also have the ability to heal. Jesus encouraged us to replenish our bodies with water, meditation, and prayer. He emphasized the importance of praying for those we healed, as prayer sets intentions and sends love to those who need it most.

Curious, I asked Jesus about the young girl. "Why did she shake and throw up?"

Jesus smiled and said, "She was being healed, and her soul was also healing her. The blackness in her intestines needed to leave her body, and it was better that it did. People will talk about the healing that took place tonight. We should expect more to attend our campfire ceremonies, including city officials who will want to learn what we are doing. Rebbi Uyo will also be visiting. Go now and replenish your bodies. I need to be with God and the heavens alone. Rest in peace and many blessings."

Before I closed my eyes to meditate, I watched as Jesus walked away from the camp. Later, I was startled awake by the sound of my name. I suddenly sat up to find Jesus kneeling beside me.

"Sarah, will you come with me?"

"I told him, "Of course."

It was dark, with only the stars and the moon providing light. We hadn't brought a candle.

We walked down a small hill, and he reassured me not to be afraid. He wanted me to meet someone who helps guide him, explaining that this guidance comes from another star. Although I had many questions, I felt surprisingly safe, and my curiosity took over. "God doesn't guide you?"

Jesus said, "Yes. God guides me, but he also brings me another source to help not only me but mankind. God made many stars and many heavenly bodies. We are part of God's plans."

Suddenly, I saw a figure bathed in light. Jesus explained his guide speaks through thoughts and instructed me to take a deep breath.

As I continued to gaze at this radiant being, a gentle voice spoke to me: "Sarah, it's a pleasure to meet you. Jesus has spoken highly of you. Your heart is pure, and you will assist him on his mission. We will ensure the safety of his wife and family. As his journey grows more dangerous, Jesus will require a female presence by his side.

God has ordained harmony between male and female. Your spiritual name will be Mary, for you remind Jesus of his mother, who also had a pure heart and embraced her role in this sacred mission. Mankind will be forever changed by Jesus. Do you accept this quest?"

"I do." I answered before I had a chance to really think about it. I asked, " Will you also help guide me?"

I was told that Jesus would guide me. Curious, I asked if it knew the future. The light being explained that many futures are written, and while Earth operates within the bounds of time, other stars do not. It reassured me that answers would come when the time was right. Naturally, I still had many questions.

"Remember that love is always the answer."

Suddenly, I was sitting up on my bed at the camp. Jesus was sitting next to me, smiling.

"We will talk more tomorrow. Please do not repeat to anyone what took place. This experience was for you and you alone." I was about to say something, but found myself in a deep sleep.

The bright sunlight woke me up. I could feel the warmth of the rays. Suddenly, I remembered the events that took place. I was a little confused. I knew I had met the light being, but how did I end up back at the camp? My sweet sister Shaloma sat next to me.

"Mary, it's about time you woke up. We need to clean and get dressed to go into town."

I met her eyes and asked, "Did you just call me Mary?"

She laughed and commented, "Wow, that was a good sleep. Don't even remember your spiritual name that was given to you. Let's go, Mary."

How did she know the name that was given to me the night before? The light being did tell me that it was my spiritual name. I felt that I was no longer the person, Sarah. How could this be? Sarah was my human name, given by my parents.

Shaloma and I went into town, and I noticed that everyone was calling me Mary. I felt like a bird taking flight for the first time, as if I were beginning a new life—a new spiritual life. As I spoke with people in town, I began to see a glow surrounding their bodies. However, a few had a darker glow around them. I asked Shaloma if she could see the light glow around people, but the look of confusion on her face gave me my answer.

"Mary, are you still sleeping?"

I laughed and told her, "No, I'm more awake than I was yesterday."

I felt drawn to the people who had a darker glow to them. I told them about the camp and how Jesus would heal not only with his words but with his body, his hands. He healed everyone's mind, body, and soul.

Many would throw their hands up and tell me it was blasphemy and that I should be ashamed. They also told me to sacrifice a goat to the gods so that they would forgive me for my nasty ways. As they were abusing me with their words, I quietly sent them my loving energy. This is what Jesus taught us.

Not everyone will accept our generous energy in words, but you don't know if you are planting a seed into their hearts to produce a flower that will bloom and smell like the heavens.

Shaloma pulled me towards a tree. "Mary, let's take a break." She pulled some fruit from her sachet and handed me one.

"Thank you, sweet friend."

She told me she was worried about me and asked why I approached the people in town who were verbally abusive.

"I would have just walked away, but you stayed and listened and took this abuse."

I found the words to explain to her that I know I'm doing God's work and that He is empowering me to continue reaching out to those who need it most. Everyone is on their own journey, facing different challenges. Yes, we may feel alone at times, but there are certain lessons we must each learn. I hope that our efforts will   inspire others to empower one another.

Shaloma looked at me with a knowing grin. "Mary, you sound just like Jesus."

"Well, I do walk beside him, don't I? And you will too. Jesus's words will flow through all of us."

As we left town, I noticed a few men following us. I urged Shaloma to quicken her pace as my heart began to race, making it hard to catch my breath. I whispered a small prayer for our safety. We were only halfway back when the men drew closer. Shaloma held my hand tightly. Just then, I saw someone approaching us from ahead —it was Jesus. He called out, greeting us warmly. The men suddenly stopped in their tracks and turned around. Jesus tried to get their attention, but they ignored him.

He smiled at us reassuringly. "I'm glad to see both of you. Mary, I heard your prayer, so I thought I would meet you halfway. Always follow your instincts and your intuition."

As Jesus walked with us, he told us a story. "When I was younger, I met an older man who had no home and traveled from town to town. He approached me one day while I was making a metal bowl for my mother. He seemed friendly, with a huge smile that put me at ease. As I worked, he began sharing stories about his adventurous life. Just then, my younger sister appeared at the door to tell me dinner was ready. The moment she stepped into the doorway, I sensed danger.

A whisper in my head warned me that we were not safe—it felt as if God himself was telling me, and I listened.I told my sister that I wouldn't be long, but first, I needed to say goodbye to my new friend.

The man's smile faded as he gazed at me. 'Can I not stay for dinner? I thought you would be a good host.'

I told him that I could offer him some bread, but it was best for him to continue on his adventure. I could sense his anger and aggression building. As I started to walk out of my shop, he grabbed one of my tools. I calmly asked him to put it down, but instead, he swung it at me. I had no choice but to strike him in the stomach. He dropped the tool and said he would leave.

As he began to walk up the hill behind our house, I quickly grabbed the bread and ran after him.

'Brother, here's your bread.'

He appeared shocked. ' You still give me bread after my hostility towards you?'

I handed him the bread and gently told him to take it, assuring him that I would pray for his safe travels. He began to cry and asked why I would do this. I explained that prayers are an expression of love and that I forgave him. While I needed to keep my family safe, I reminded him that we are all brothers—we are one. Everyone makes decisions based on what they are learning.

Mary & Shaloma always follow your instincts; they will keep you safe."

When we returned to camp, Jesus asked if we could talk in private. We walked over to my favorite tree. He began to speak, and I found myself hanging on every word, fully immersed in what he was saying.

"I want to thank you for saying yes to your new spiritual life and mission. I hope you don't mind your new spiritual name, Mary."

I told him that I felt honored to be chosen to work alongside him, and I could feel the love from the heavens. I had never experienced such peace and serenity before. My human name, Sarah, would always be a part of me and remain in my heart, but my new name, Mary, made me feel closer to God. Curious, I asked him how everyone knew my new name. He smiled and explained that the heavens had rewritten our daily reality.

"Everything was renewed and everyone remembers you as Mary. They also remember you as my partner, my wife."

I gasped. "I'm your wife?"

Jesus held my hand. "Do you remember the light being?"

I shook my head yes.

"This light being is helping me, along with several other spiritual beings that God has sent to assist with my mission. The light being told me that I would be more successful and better received in the Jewish community if I had a wife. You are my spiritual wife. As I've mentioned, I have a human wife and family who are being kept safe, and you will be kept safe as well. There's no need for a traditional wife relationship between us. This is a spiritual bond, and it doesn't need to follow earthly traditions."

For once, I was speechless. "So, everyone remembers us being husband and wife?"

"Yes, they remember your past. Soon after we met, everyone remembers that we had a celebration and you became my wife."

I could feel angels hugging me. I said, "As it is written, it shall be."

As we walked back to the center of camp, I began to see things differently. Feeling dizzy, I had to sit near the fire. I could see energy waves moving through the camp, with everyone vibrating with energy. I could look into their souls and even hear their thoughts. It was overwhelming, yet incredibly beautiful.

Jesus sat next to me and held my hand. "Mary, breathe into it."

I told him it was beautiful. "Am I dead?"

Jesus laughed. "No, you are awake, not dead."

"I can feel what everyone is experiencing, both their thoughts and emotions. I can even sense the tree we sat under and the warmth and love from Mother Earth. I can see the energy flowing around us and through us. We are all connected to this energy, and we are all connected to each other. That's what you meant when you said we are all one."

Jesus said, "Yes, we are all one—one with God in the heavens. Earth was created so that we could take on a different form, becoming human, to learn and grow. This is why I needed to experience life as a human child, to understand what it means to be human. We are all wearing a human suit, temporarily forgetting who we truly are so that we can learn. When we are ready, we reopen that part of our spiritual selves. I'm here to help mankind deepen its spirituality.

Whatever happens, it is meant to be. Mary, you were chosen to be with me at this time because you, too, will make a significant impact. You will learn how to turn off your spiritual senses so that you can fulfill your role as a human. When you want to access these senses or when you need to turn them off, you can do so by willingly closing your eyes. Take a deep breath, slow down your energy. Now, open your eyes. Things will return to how they were before."

I told him that I liked seeing the energy.

"But you also said I needed to see things as others do so that I could relate to them as a human."

Jesus reassured me that I would know when to turn on my spiritual senses. I felt immense gratitude for being shown how things truly look—so angelic and beautiful.

Reflections on Chapter 6

1. Sarah's transformation into Mary is marked by a new spiritual identity and purpose. How does this name change symbolize her spiritual rebirth and new role in Jesus' mission?

2. The encounter with the light being introduces the concept of guidance from celestial beings. How does this expand your understanding of divine guidance and the interconnectedness of the universe?

3. Jesus explains the significance of Mary as his "spiritual wife" to aid his mission within the Jewish community. How does this spiritual partnership challenge or reinforce your understanding of relationships and roles in a spiritual context?

4. Mary begins to see the energy and interconnectedness of all beings and nature. How does this newfound ability to perceive spiritual energy impact her understanding of the world around her? What does this suggest about the nature of reality?

5. The chapter touches on the idea that humans are spiritual beings having a human experience. How does this perspective influence your view on the purpose of life and the challenges we face as human beings?

6. Jesus teaches Mary how to "turn on" and "turn off" her spiritual senses. What might be the spiritual significance of being able to navigate between heightened spiritual awareness and ordinary human perception?

7. Throughout the chapter, there is a strong emphasis on unity and oneness with God, nature, and each other. How does this theme of oneness resonate with your own spiritual beliefs or practices?

8. Throughout the chapter, there is a strong emphasis on unity and oneness with God, nature, and each other. How does this theme of oneness resonate with your own spiritual beliefs or practices?

9. The chapter highlights the concept of divine timing and the unfolding of multiple possible futures. How does this idea of a non-linear or multi-faceted future affect your understanding of destiny, free will, and spiritual growth?

10. Mary experiences an overwhelming sense of gratitude for being shown the true nature of reality. How does gratitude function as a spiritual practice in your life, and how might it help in navigating both human and spiritual challenges?

Chapter 7:
The Gift of Healing

O ver time, I adjusted to my life in the role of Mary. The others not only accepted me as Jesus' wife but also recognized me as a spiritual guide. I had the opportunity to speak to small groups around the fire after Jesus shared his teachings. Each time I spoke, I felt heaven speaking through me, and I could sense that everyone in the circle needed to hear what I was sharing. They listened to every word as if it were sacred—and indeed, it was.

Being a woman was challenging, but with the support of Jesus and the heavens, it became possible. I primarily gathered with women in my group. They craved the nourishment that the words provided— hope, peace, and love. They longed to be seen for who they truly were, and their souls needed replenishment. During the day, they were treated like property, but at night, they felt whole and special.

One day, an angry husband confronted us. He was upset about the changes he saw in his wife and demanded to know what we were doing to her. He wanted his old wife back and was determined to find out who this teacher was and who Mary was. Jesus remained patient, listening calmly until the man had finished.

Then, Jesus simply asked him, 'Do you love your wife?'

The man shrugged in response. "Of course, she is a big asset to our family."

Jesus then shared his thoughts. "When flowers bloom, they need nourishment and sunlight to thrive. Your wife is like a flower—she keeps your family strong, shares her essence with you, and brings beauty to your home. To keep her petals strong and vibrant, she needs spiritual nourishment. Why don't you join us tonight?"

The man was surprised that Jesus wasn't angry; in fact, the kindness in Jesus' words seemed to irritate him even more.

"No, I won't be here and neither will my wife."

Jesus gently told him to go in love, offering a blessing for him and his family. My heart sank, knowing that his wife would likely not return. As I struggled with this realization, Jesus looked at me.

"Mary, don't be sad. You don't know what seeds we've planted, not just in his wife but in him as well. Everyone is free, with their own free will. They must make their own choices, and they can only heal spiritually if they are willing to accept that healing. Pray for him and his family, and send loving energy their way. Go and rest now. Tonight, more will come—lost sheep in need of a shepherd to help guide them."

I was forever grateful that the heavens had sent us Jesus. The world—my world, my community—needed him desperately. He brought love, hope, and, most of all, miracles. The evening of healing was beautiful.

As we assisted Jesus, I tuned into my spiritual senses and could see the energy circling around the camp and flowing through each of us. One gentleman came seeking healing, brought by his two daughters. They explained to Jesus that something had changed in him—he had become more angry and violent. As he stepped forward, I gasped. While his energy held some light, there was also a dark energy within him, stagnant and unmoving. Jesus placed his hands on the man's shoulders and closed his eyes, asking us to place our hands on his back. We honored this man through our own light language, and as we did, he fell to his knees. Suddenly, the darkness began to shift, and the man vomited as the darkness left his body.

Jesus then said,"We give the darkness to God."

I saw black smoke suddenly leave the man's mouth, rising straight to the heavens. In an instant, a light appeared in the heavens, engulfing the darkness. The man began to cry, thanking us and Jesus.

He kissed Jesus' hands repeatedly, but Jesus gently motioned for him to stand.

"Go and live,' Jesus told him, 'and do not bow down to the earth's troubles.' Then, Jesus raised his arms. 'When you live in fear or anger, illness follows. Whatever you feel, whatever you feed your body, will manifest in your life. Treat your body as a sacred vessel. Purify it with stillness and prayers. Your body has energy centers, and its energy should flow like a river. However, this flow can be blocked by dark energies if the light within you is diminished. Nurture your energy centers with love and kindness. Remember, only you can decide how to respond to the challenges of this world. God has given you free will, and we are all connected as one. If a brother or sister is ill, we are all affected. Help one another. Pray not only for those you love but also for your enemies. God knows your heart, and your soul knows it too. Allow everyone to be who they are. Society gives us rules to follow, often to keep us safe, but sometimes those rules are about control. That's why I am here—to wake everyone up so they can see the true light of this world. Lessons are being learned, and choices are being made.Sometimes we don't understand why things happen, why good people die, but this is where faith and love come in."

As Jesus was talking, I could see energy surrounding him. The lights swirled up to the heavens and exploded above the camp. It rained light energy around us.

Jesus ended by saying, "Let's celebrate each other through food and dance." Everyone clapped, and it felt wonderful to dance and celebrate with my brothers and sisters. The stars seemed brighter than ever that night. Jesus was an incredible dancer, and it was heartwarming to see him laugh and enjoy himself—embracing his humanity. Everyone wanted to be near him. After our guests departed, Jesus sat down with his closest followers.

"Brothers and sisters, it is time for us to move on. We need to reach those living outside of town; they too need to hear our message of hope and love. We may need to split into smaller groups and establish a central camp. Get some rest, for we will be leaving tomorrow."

I felt a deep sadness knowing I would be leaving the town where I had grown up, leaving behind my friend Mary. The memories —both good and bad—would remain forever in my heart. As everyone settled down to sleep, Jesus approached me and said he would be meeting with the light being, urging me to get some rest. My eyes grew heavy as I watched him walk away into the darkness.

I awoke to the sound of Paul and Simon laughing. The sun was shining, and it promised to be a good day for travel.

When we asked Jesus where we were headed, he simply smiled and said, "Where the heart wants to go. God will show us the way."

We still used the cart I once used to transport my pottery. Maybe someday, I'll be able to make pottery again. I made sure Jesus took the figurines that had been given to him and his earthly wife; he always kept them safely in his sachet. I had nothing tangible to hold onto, only the memories in my heart. So, we walked together, following Jesus. Somehow, we always had enough food and water for everyone.

As we walked, we came across an older gentleman who appeared abandoned and unable to walk. He asked us for food, and Jesus responded by asking if we could stop and pray with him. The man nodded, saying that the company would be good. Jesus placed his hands on the man's head, and we surrounded him, joining in the healing.

Even in the daylight, I could see the energy moving—it always began with Jesus. As he prayed, the energy flowed into the man, then connected with us like a string of light, interweaving us together before ascending to the heavens. The man grew stronger and began to cry, telling Jesus that he had nothing to give in return. Jesus simply told him to share what had happened today with others.

He then asked me to retrieve a small basket and a water jug from the cart. Handing the basket to the man, Jesus told him to hold it. The man shrugged, saying it was empty. Jesus smiled and was now full of bread and figs.

"This basket is like life." Jesus continued, "Be excited about life, even when it seems empty, because one day it can be filled with miracles, love, and hope. Eat, replenish, and live your life in blessings. Today, we have learned that humans are capable of healing others through prayer and energy."

Witnessing Jesus heal was always a revelation. His entire being radiated with a divine glow, his grace a vivid testament to the boundless love of God. Each time, it struck me deeply—the pulsing energy of pure love that seemed to animate him served as a powerful reminder that we are all fragments of that same infinite energy. As we journeyed forward, the sunlight waned, casting long shadows on our path, and Jesus, sensing the right moment, gestured for us to halt and set up camp for the night. No sooner had we started our preparations than we were approached by a small group, a quiet child at its heart.

Jesus, with a tenderness that seemed to reach beyond the physical realm, shared with me his fondness for healing children.

"They are the heralds of a new dawn," he would say, emphasizing their role in spreading the word of his teachings.

The child's father was forthright about their plight, but it was the mother's anxious eyes that spoke volumes of their distress.

"Our daughter has lost her voice," the father explained, his voice heavy with worry. "She doesn't even look at us anymore, just stares into the distance, barely eating enough to sustain herself."

Jesus, moved by the child's condition, beckoned her forward gently. With a solemnity reserved for such moments, he instructed us to keep our distance and immerse ourselves in prayer. From his sachet, he retrieved two wooden statues—a likeness of him and his earthly wife, which he placed in the child's small hands. As he whispered in the ancient light language, his hands not touching but hovering just above her head, I witnessed their energies intertwine, glowing and pulsating with a growing intensity.

After a moment that seemed both fleeting and eternal, Jesus paused and softly encouraged the child, "Open your eyes; you are safe, surrounded by love."

To our collective relief, the girl did more than just open her eyes —she smiled, her first words a whispered "Thank you" that brought tears to her parents' eyes.

Overwhelmed with gratitude, they asked how they could possibly repay him. Jesus, with his customary humility, requested only that they share their story with others and join us for dinner, an invitation they accepted with honor.

During the meal, Jesus learned the child's name—Kathleena— and when she attempted to return the wooden figures, he insisted she keep them.

"Always play, be creative, and let your imagination guide you," he told her, watching with a soft smile as she delighted in her new treasures.

As the evening drew to a close, weariness enveloping us all, even Jesus among the chorus of snores, I lay thinking about the profound simplicity of his

gifts—not just the tangible figurines to Kathleena but the gift of hope and healing he bestowed upon everyone he met.

Reflections on Chapter 7

1. Mary's role as both Jesus' wife and a spiritual guide to other women is significant. How does this dual role illustrate the importance of female leadership in spiritual communities, particularly in the context of this story?

2. The healing sessions described in this chapter involve a deep connection between physical and spiritual energies. How does the depiction of these healings enhance your understanding of the relationship between the body, mind, and spirit?

3. Jesus' interaction with the angry husband highlights the tension between societal norms and spiritual growth. How does Jesus' response to the husband's anger reflect the spiritual principle of love and patience, even in the face of hostility?

4. The chapter describes a moment where Mary sees dark energy being released from a man during a healing session. How does this imagery of dark and light energies contribute to the chapter's overall message about spiritual cleansing and transformation?

5. Jesus speaks about the importance of nurturing one's body and soul to maintain spiritual health. How does this advice resonate with your own practices for maintaining balance and harmony in your life?

6. The transformation of the young girl, Kathleena, from a silent, withdrawn state to one of joy and gratitude is a powerful moment. What does this healing symbolize in terms of the power of love and faith in overcoming darkness?

7. Mary experiences the divine energy and light surrounding Jesus during the healing sessions. How does her ability to see and feel this energy deepen her spiritual journey and understanding of her role in the community?

8. The chapter explores the idea of planting seeds of love and hope in others, even if the immediate impact is not visible. How does this concept of "planting seeds" align with the spiritual practice of faith and patience in witnessing growth over time?

9. Jesus emphasizes the importance of free will and the personal choice to accept or reject spiritual healing. How does this respect for individual autonomy reflect broader spiritual principles of freedom and responsibility?

10. The chapter ends with a sense of community and shared purpose, as Jesus and his followers prepare to move on to a new place. How does this ongoing journey represent the continuous process of spiritual growth and the spreading of light in the world?

Chapter 8:

Threads of Destiny

With the dawn, our journey resumed, buoyed by the addition of those we had healed, including the man from earlier. Each new follower brought their own story, their own seeking spirit, and as our numbers grew, so did the noticeable sense of purpose among us. Jesus reminded us often of the importance of our experiences, urging us to remember and share the lessons we learned, to nurture the seed of knowledge planted in our hearts that we might help it—and our understanding—reach towards the heavens.

Each step with Jesus was a lesson in faith, a demonstration of love's transformative power. As I listened to the stories of why each follower had come—some out of curiosity, some in desperate need—I was daily grateful for the privilege of witnessing these spiritual unfoldings, participating in a movement that seemed destined to reshape the world.

As night fell and we prepared our numerous fires to accommodate our expanded numbers, Jesus shared a quiet reflection that resonated deeply: the path of spiritual awakening is fraught with challenges, yet filled with the profound joy of discovery and connection. In his company, every moment was a step towards eternity, a dance with the divine orchestrated by the most humble of masters who walked among us as both guide and guardian.

I will never forget the profoundness of Jesus' message that night. He shared with us the paradox of our mission: the more people learned about these spiritual events, the more dangerous our path would become. Jesus was igniting hope, a flame so powerful that it threatened those who wished to control society through fear and oppression. He gently prepared us for his impending departure, reminding us to hold faith despite the uncertainties ahead.

"Remember, my time with you in this form is shortening, but remember also that I am not just with you as a man walking beside you —I am and will always be part of the love within your hearts," he told us, his voice imbued with both melancholy and resolve.

He urged us to see that we were all fragments of the divine, capable of shaping our destinies with the free will granted by God. The silence that followed was profound, filled with the weight of what was to come. As we prepared for the night, Jesus grasped my hand reassuringly, his touch a bastion of comfort.

"It'll be okay. Pray whenever you need guidance," he assured me.

That night, my sleep was restless, disturbed by visions of the path unfolding before us.

The next morning was solemn for all, a quiet where each of us contemplated the future. Jesus often instructed us to live in the moment, to truly experience and appreciate our current existence rather than get lost in what was to come. Taking this to heart, I resolved to cherish every remaining moment with him and bolster his spiritual mission with all my energy.

As we packed up to continue our journey, I felt a strong urge to gather everyone for a collective prayer. Even Jesus joined us, standing quietly among his followers. I led them in a prayer of gratitude for the lessons Jesus had imparted, for his presence that had irrevocably changed our lives.

"Though we may not understand the entirety of God's plan, we trust that the heavens will guide us and provide the strength we need to persevere," I prayed. "Even if Jesus no longer walks the earth with us, his spirit will remain intertwined with ours, guiding us from a realm we are yet to see."

The prayer seemed to lift spirits, infusing the group with a renewed sense of purpose and joy. With hearts lighter, we resumed our mission to spread the message of hope and love. Throughout that day, every encounter with weary souls along the road seemed to affirm our purpose. The oppressed left us standing a little taller, touched by the healing power of Jesus' words and the energy we shared.

That evening, under the stars and around the fire, Jesus prepared us for another revelation.

"There is always hope and boundless love available to us. God wishes us to lead fulfilled and abundant lives, but we must be awake to experience this," he began, his voice stirring the cool night air. "We often go through life half asleep, adhering to societal rules that dampen our spirit and confine our hearts. Miracles happen every day, but we do not witness these miracles since we are asleep. Pay attention and embrace these miracles. See with your physical eyes, see with your third eye, see with your heart. One of these miracles I'm going to show you today, we are not alone on earth. Yes, we have the animals, bugs, plants, water, air, and dirt, but the heavens are always with you. We even have people from the stars around us."

Suddenly, the atmosphere shifted, and several ethereal figures of light appeared around us. Jesus explained that these beings from the stars were here to aid us, part of a divine network supporting our journey. I approached one of these beings, drawn by a familiar sensation of warmth.

As it transformed into a more human-like form before me, it greeted me, "Hello, Sarah, known as Mary."

Curious, I asked why it had come.

The being explained, "We are here to assist in fulfilling your spiritual mission. We guide and teach you what you need during your time on Earth, but we do so without interfering with your free will. Each of you has a spiritual team to help you learn and grow throughout your earthly journey. When you are born into this realm, you know everyone in your spiritual team, but as the human body grows and changes, it is in your DNA and energy points to forget your true self. Remembering all your lifetimes and feeling the full power of your energy would be too overwhelming for your human body. As you become more spiritual, you recall what is necessary to fulfill your lessons, though you won't remember everything. This is why you have a spiritual team—to help guide you. You chose who would be on your team before you were born. Everyone you encounter on the earthly plane, you have known for many lifetimes under the stars. Your story is still unfolding, a tapestry being woven together. Each thread is connected, and if one becomes weak, the tapestry can unravel. This is why it's crucial to have a spiritual team to help guide you and keep your story strong as it continues to be created. Your story exists on many tapestries, with threads interwoven across multiple realms. You are here, but you are also in other dimensions, playing out different choices. In one lifetime, you may have chosen not to visit Jesus at the campfire, and your story unfolded without him. Yet, it is all part of one collective narrative. These stories unite us, weaving together our shared existence as one. All of these stories and their energies are gathered in a place within the heavenly realm, a place you will be able to see once you transition back to your trueself. You have traveled to many places under the stars, Mary, and many on your spiritual team come from different realms as well. When you look up at the stars, you see only a fraction of what truly exists. In this vast universe, anything is possible."

Grasping the magnitude of the teachings from the light being was challenging yet deeply transformative. I requested a few silent moments with them—a sacred pause in our spiritual communion. As we sat quietly, the golden light bathed me in peace. Around the camp, each follower was deep in their own spiritual dialogue, a serene tableau under the starlit sky. Even Jesus was meditative, his presence a calm anchor in the swirling energies. During this profound silence, I experienced an extraordinary sense of clarity.

Though my eyes were closed, I perceived the vibrant life energy weaving through each person around me, a luminous dance of interconnected spirits. It was as if I could see with more than my eyes; my heart and soul were open, attuned to the profound truths being revealed.

In this heightened state, I asked what name I should use for them. They responded that they had many names, but it was up to me to choose one that resonated deeply.

Instantly, I knew: Hokama, a name that had always held a special place in my heart. Curious, I asked why I was drawn to choose them over another. Hokama explained that our souls recognize each other by the unique frequency each of us emits, and theirs aligned perfectly with mine.

Before our time together ended, Hokama transformed, taking on the youthful and vibrant form of my earthly father. His appearance startled me into tears—not of sorrow, but of overwhelming love.

"Child, do not cry," he soothed, his voice a comforting balm. "Our time together is eternal, transcending the mere physical. I am here to show you that life is merely a series of transitions, a journey of the soul through various states of being. Remember, whatever unfolds on Earth is part of a greater script, one written in the stars. Trust in this process and stand firm in your truth."

With these parting words, his light dimmed and he vanished, leaving me in a state of awe and gratitude. I returned to my bed, emotionally spent yet spiritually fulfilled. Around me, others continued their engagements with their spiritual guides, while Jesus remained in deep contemplation.

I looked up at the stars, thanking them for the profound connections and revelations of the night. The scent of white flowers, reminiscent of those near my childhood home, filled the air as I drifted into sleep.

Reflections on Chapter 8

1. Mary's encounter with the light beings emphasizes the idea of a spiritual team that guides us throughout our lives. How does this concept resonate with your own beliefs about spiritual guidance and the role of unseen forces in our lives?

2. The chapter describes life as a tapestry, with each thread representing a different choice or experience. How does this metaphor shape your understanding of destiny, free will, and the interconnectedness of our experiences?

3. Jesus' reminder that his time in physical form is limited yet his presence remains within the hearts of his followers reflects a deep spiritual truth. How does this idea of an eternal spiritual presence impact your view on loss and the continuity of relationships beyond the physical realm?

4. The light being tells Mary that she is living multiple realities simultaneously, with each choice creating a different thread in the tapestry of her life. How does this perspective challenge or enhance your understanding of the nature of reality and the spiritual implications of our choices?

5. Mary's spiritual journey in this chapter is marked by a deepening connection with her true self and the divine. How does this progression reflect the broader themes of spiritual awakening and the journey towards self-realization?

6. The chapter highlights the importance of recognizing and embracing miracles in our everyday lives. How can this practice of spiritual mindfulness change the way we perceive and experience the world around us?

7. Hokama, the light being, explains that our souls recognize each other by unique frequencies. How does this concept of soul frequencies and spiritual alignment influence your understanding of relationships and connections with others?

8. Mary experiences a profound sense of clarity and interconnectedness during her encounter with the light beings. How does this moment of spiritual insight contribute to the overall message of unity and oneness in the chapter?

9. The chapter touches on the idea that our earthly life is just one part of a greater spiritual journey. How does this belief affect the way you approach challenges and experiences in your own life?

10. Mary's encounter with her father in the form of a light being emphasizes the eternal nature of love and connection. How does this reunion shape your understanding of the afterlife and the enduring bonds we share with loved ones?

Chapter 9:
The Eternal Journey

The following morning, Jesus greeted us with a hearty breakfast, and shared that each of our experiences that night was unique. He urged us to hold these memories close, as personal treasures of our spiritual journey. Soon, he revealed, his mother would join us, bringing even more followers to our ever-growing circle.

As the days passed, our camp had to relocate to accommodate the increasing number of seekers. I found myself deeply engaged in healing and teaching, especially with the women who arrived, burdened by life yet eager for spiritual solace. Their stories of struggle and resilience added layers to our shared experience, each narrative enriching the tapestry of our communal life.

The day came when Jesus' mother, Mary, arrived at the camp. Her presence was a soothing force, her understanding of Jesus' mission profound and nurturing. She became a mother figure to me as well, offering strength and wisdom as we navigated the complexities of our path.

Yet, amidst our spiritual enrichment, the reality of our mission's danger loomed. The day the guards came to arrest Jesus marked a pivotal moment. His mother and I held each other, our tears a mixture of grief and grace, feeling the protective embrace of angels amidst the turmoil. It was a stark reminder of the harsh world outside our spiritual haven, where a man of peace faced hostility and violence.

As Jesus' earthly journey reached its cruel climax, I was there beside him, witnessing the profound sacrifice he made. Even in his final moments, as life ebbed from him and he was nailed to the cross, his face bloodied and marred, he looked heavenward and smiled—a poignant affirmation of his unwavering faith and the eternal nature of his spirit.

His essence is pure love, meant to uplift and guide us spiritually. He is intertwined with our very being, and we with him.

While each of us may follow a different God, engage with diverse spiritual guides, or look to various celestial beings, this diversity is by divine design. Jesus was specifically chosen by the heavens to fulfill a critical spiritual mission—to offer us guidance and hope, to teach us the ways of love, and to help us seek our truths and deepen our spiritual understanding.

After Jesus ascended, I had the solemn duty of tending to his body, assisting in its cleansing as he had spiritually cleansed me. Alongside me were the men who had perished with him, and I aided in their cleansing too. I was struck by awe, yet not surprised, when Jesus' physical form vanished; it was a fitting epitaph to his earthly narrative. But his story did not end with his disappearance. He returned to visit us, manifesting not as a spectral figure but in the full likeness of a man, altering his appearance to meet us in forms we most needed for our understanding and comfort. Many did not recognize him initially, because he appeared differently, showing us that even in spirit, our journey of transformation and learning continues. He taught us that as we depart this earth, we carry with us the lessons of a lifetime, the freedom to choose our paths, and a spiritual flame that endures eternally.

In these profound moments and encounters, Jesus emphasized a crucial truth: our existence is a tapestry of growth and evolution, where each experience, each choice, is a thread in the ever-expanding fabric of the universe. His continued presence in various forms was a testament to the ongoing journey of the soul beyond the physical realm —a journey that he still guides, as we navigate the complexities of our spiritual evolutions, forever alight with the eternal flame of divine love and wisdom.

His legacy, however, would endure beyond his physical departure. His teachings, his essence would permeate the ages, influencing countless souls. To some, he would be a divine figure; to others, a spiritual master; and yet to others, simply a man whose life exemplified unconditional love and profound spiritual truth.

In the aftermath, as his followers and I continued to spread his teachings, we faced trials and tribulations, but Jesus' peace was with us, guiding us through each challenge. I dedicated myself to chronicling these teachings, aware that while my name might fade into obscurity, the essence of my spirit, connected to the divine, would continue to evolve and transcend across lifetimes and realms.

Thus, I, Sarah, who walked among Jesus, bearing witness to a profound journey of faith, love, and transformation that forever changed the course of my soul and the souls of those around me. I am.

Reflections on Chapter 9

1. How does the arrival of Jesus' mother, Mary, influence the spiritual dynamics of the camp? What does her presence symbolize in the context of the group's mission and the challenges they face?

2. Jesus' crucifixion and subsequent appearances in different forms after his resurrection are pivotal moments in this chapter. How do these events shape your understanding of the concepts of sacrifice, resurrection, and eternal life in spiritual teachings?

3. The chapter emphasizes the idea that each person may follow different spiritual guides or deities, but that all are part of a divine plan. How does this inclusivity align with your own views on spiritual diversity and unity?

4. Mary's role in cleansing Jesus' body after his death parallels her own spiritual cleansing earlier in the story. How does this act of service deepen her spiritual journey, and what does it reveal about the connection between physical acts and spiritual growth?

5. Jesus' teaching that our existence is a tapestry of growth and evolution suggests that each experience and choice is meaningful. How does this metaphor resonate with your own spiritual journey, and how do you see the threads of your life contributing to the greater whole?

6. The chapter speaks to the ongoing presence of Jesus in spirit, guiding his followers even after his physical departure. How does this concept of continued spiritual guidance and presence comfort or challenge your understanding of life after death?

7. Jesus' transformation into different forms after his resurrection emphasizes the idea of continual learning and growth. How does this idea of spiritual transformation inspire you in your own life and spiritual practices?

8. The chapter explores the theme of legacy, both in terms of Jesus' teachings and Mary's commitment to chronicling them. How do you perceive the importance of preserving spiritual knowledge, and what role do you think legacy plays in spiritual evolution?

9. As Mary reflects on her journey with Jesus and the profound changes it brought to her soul, what lessons do you think are most important for us to carry forward in our own spiritual lives?

10. The chapter concludes with Mary acknowledging that while her name might fade, the essence of her spirit connected to the divine will continue to evolve. How does this perspective influence your view on the impermanence of life and the enduring nature of the soul?

Sarah's Final Reflections-
The Light of Oneness

My story was so special to me. Jesus is known in different ways to others. He was a messiah, Christ, an ascended master, and just a human. For me, Jesus was my spiritual partner, my soulmate, the other part of my heart, which is my soul. He was so strong, stubborn, and loving. He had a spiritual mission to fulfill. He showed humankind how life continues, how we are a part of him, God, and the universe. The candle cannot be lit without everyone. We are the flame. We are the warmth. We are the everlasting light. Jesus changed our societies, our earth, and us.

I wanted to use my earthly name, Sarah, for my story and for my teachings. My spiritual name is dear to my heart, but many on earth will worship the name Mary. My purpose for my teachings is for everyone to know that as I walked among Jesus, I was a human with everyday earthly problems. And yes, as a woman, Jesus allowed me to teach around the campfire. The Holy Spirit radiated through me. We are this spirit. Through this heavenly spirit, we can all be and live as Jesus did. We can create miracles. These come in small or big packages. Remember what Jesus said about my small wine pitcher. He told me that this small size meant that it would be used for bigger things.

My current teachings are just now beginning. It is time. People in the present are lost. They know there is more spiritual knowledge to learn. Religion has its purpose. The earth's energy is rising to a new enlightenment. People are awakening. The process can be fulfilling but can bring chaos to life. Everyone needs each other. Everyone will begin to remember who they are, not only in this lifetime but throughout their own soul's history.

My lessons will be about truth, wisdom, and love. These elements will help others find what they seek. As I speak, I will speak and touch everyone's soul. The energy that I bring from the heavens will be a beacon of light that they will need on their spiritual journey. May you find your soul's light. This light will shine bright enough and radiate enough to reach the light of oneness.

Forever light and love,
Sarah/Mary

Wisdom & Love- Jesus Reflects on Sarah's Life

I remember the first time I met Sarah. I was walking through the market, spreading my teachings and inviting others to join me. Not many people knew me, though they had heard my name. As I wandered through the bustling market, a display of beautiful pottery caught my eye. The symbols on the pottery drew me closer, and that's when I noticed a young woman standing beside them. I remember the first time I met Sarah. I was walking through the market, spreading my teachings and inviting others to join me. Not many people knew me, though they had heard my name. As I wandered through the bustling market, a display of beautiful pottery caught my eye. The symbols on the pottery drew me closer, and that's when I noticed a young woman standing beside them.

Curious about the symbols, I approached her. At first, she avoided my gaze, seemingly afraid. I spoke to her gently, hoping to ease her fear, and slowly, she began to feel safe. I asked her why she created such beautiful pottery.

She looked up at me and smiled, saying, "I make it because it brings joy to others.

" I shook my head gently and asked again, "Why do you make pottery?"

She paused, then replied, "I start with the clay, and it becomes something that comes from my heart."

I then asked her about the symbols on the pottery.

She smiled again and said, "I have always been drawn to the triangle. It even appears in my dreams."

I asked for her name, and though I initially heard it as Mary, she corrected me, "My name is Sarah. Would you like to buy some pottery?"

I explained that while I appreciated her work, I traveled often and couldn't carry it with me. She asked which piece was my favorite, and I pointed to a small wine pitcher. She told me her father also loved the small wine pitchers.

I told her about our gatherings around the campfire, where we shared teachings and fellowship. In my heart, I knew that Sarah, this young woman, would offer much in the spiritual journey ahead. I continued to walk through the market until it was time to get ready for the festivities at the campfire. The marketplace was my favorite place to share with others about our festivities.

At the campfire, people are searching for things. When they go to the market, their hearts are open to new information.

Later, as I prepared for the evening's festivities at the campfire, I saw two young women approaching, laughing as if they didn't have a care in the world. Their energy was pure and innocent, like children eager to learn. One of them was Sarah, and she introduced her friend, Mary. Sarah was carrying the small wine pitcher. I asked her to give it to Matthew to place on the giving table.

As the evening unfolded, I watched Sarah and Mary integrate into the gathering. The energy they brought was angelic, a rare gift in a gathering where men often outnumbered women. Many who attended were seeking to be heard, and Sarah's questions and curiosity opened doors for others, allowing them to see beyond what they thought was possible.

Her energy had transformed since our first meeting in the market. It had only been a few hours, but she had grown so much. When Sarah began to speak, I saw a spirit guiding her, whispering in her ear. However, when a man questioned the presence of women speaking at our gathering, I noticed the disappointment in Sarah's eyes. She longed to share her truth, but the societal norms of our time stifled her voice.

I spoke up, reminding the man that we are all one, created by God, and that both men and women had the right to speak in our camp. Our female and male energies were essential to spreading hope, peace, and love. The man, still angry, left the camp, and I felt a heaviness in my heart, sensing that this would not be the last we'd see of him.

The next morning, my fears were confirmed. Mary came to the camp in tears, shaken. She told me that Sarah had been attacked andwas lying in a pool of blood. My heart sank, and I prayed for guidance. My brothers and I rushed to Sarah's home, and I asked that only Mary and I enter.

I knelt beside Sarah, who, though injured, still radiated light.

Angels and other spirits surrounded her. I prayed and channeled energy to help her heal, and as I did, I saw her soul smile at me.

I knew that from this day forward, Sarah's life would change. This near-death experience would elevate her soul to a higher level, deepening her spiritual purpose. I was grateful that such a sweet soul would remain among us. I asked Mary to clean her and gather her belongings, as Sarah would not be returning home. Mary's eyes glistened with tears, understanding that while her friend would survive, she would soon embark on a new path, one that would take her away.

That evening, Sarah joined us at the campfire. Though her energy was low, she was determined to speak about the incident in a spiritual way. As she spoke, I could see the darkness lifting from her, her energy ascending to the heavens.

Everyone present was healed by her words, and the atmosphere of the campfire was transformed, uplifted as if touched by divine light.

At sunrise, Sarah's spirit radiated the Holy Spirit. After the festivities, she had many questions about my life, driven by a fiery curiosity. I answered the most important ones and told her that the rest would be revealed in her dreams. Each night after our gatherings, I would walk down a hill to pray and commune with the heavens. Light beings guided me, revealing that Sarah was the feminine aspect of my soul and that her role in our journey would become clearer with time. When Sarah met the light beings, she recognized them as if she had always known them. She wasn't surprised or afraid. It reminded me of a child discovering the world for the first time, eager to learn more.

When the light beings changed her name to Mary, I saw her energy grow stronger, as if she were preparing for a great battle.

Though she hesitated to leave behind her earthly name, she eventually accepted the change, understanding that it was part of her spiritual quest with me.

The next day , no one remembered her as Sarah. She told me that once her name changed to Mary , she felt reborn, filled with a purpose that would change the course of history.

I admired this strong and courageous woman, now called Mary, who became enlightened so quickly. Her ability to heal others was astounding, and our relationship as spiritual husband and wife became inseparable.

As time went on, Mary's role in our community grew. My followers respected her as they would their own mother, and her angelic singing and light language brought a heavenly atmosphere to our gatherings. The women who came to the camp were drawn to her, feeling safe and loved in her presence. Her role in our spiritual quest brought harmony and peace to my heart.

As my earthly mission neared its end, I began to feel sorrow, knowing that I would soon leave Mary, my family, and my brothers and sisters. I didn't want our time together to end, but I ensured that Mary would be cared for after I was gone. During my prayers, God and the angels filled me with peace, preparing me for the day the soldiers would come for me.

On that day, I saw fear in Mary's eyes as the wind blew through our hair. As I was taken away, we made eye contact, and I knew what she felt, even without words. An angel stood behind her, and as I turned away, I drew strength from her presence.

As I walked through the streets and hung on the cross, I felt Mary's energy flowing through me. When I ascended to the heavens, we made eye contact one last time. She was not just a human being; her soul shone brightly, radiating from her physical body.

My dear friends, brothers, and sisters, Sarah—who became Mary—fulfilled a vital role in the spiritual evolution of humanity, the heavens, and the universe. She made the impossible possible, even in the most difficult of times. Remember that anything is possible if you keep your light shining.

Mary always taught about truth, knowledge, and love. Let these elements guide you on your journey through life.

I will always be with you. Keep love in your heart, and may the words that Sarah and the collective have shared with you bring you guidance, healing, and love on your spiritual journey.

Go in Peace.

Jesus

Reflections on Jesus' Words About Sarah

1. In this chapter, Jesus reflects on his first encounter with Sarah and her transformation into Mary. How does this transformation symbolize the journey of spiritual awakening and the shedding of one's old self to embrace a new spiritual identity?

2. Jesus describes Sarah as the "feminine aspect of his soul." What does this statement suggest about the importance of balancing masculine and feminine energies in spiritual practices and within ourselves?

3. The chapter emphasizes the concept of spiritual partnership, with Jesus and Mary described as spiritual husband and wife. How does this partnership illustrate the power of shared spiritual missions and the impact of collective energy on spiritual growth?

4. Jesus mentions that after Sarah's name was changed to Mary, no one remembered her as Sarah. What does this signify about the power of names and identity in spiritual transformation, and how do names carry spiritual significance in your own beliefs?

5. Mary's ability to bring harmony, peace, and healing to the community is a central theme in this chapter. How does her role as a spiritual leader among women reflect the importance of female leadership in spiritual evolution?

6. As Jesus faces his crucifixion, he draws strength from Mary's presence and energy. How does this connection between them highlight the idea that spiritual support can transcend physical boundaries and continue even in the face of great challenges?

7. Jesus advises to keep love in one's heart and to let truth, knowledge, and love guide us. How can these elements serve as foundational principles in your own spiritual journey, especially during difficult times?

8. The chapter speaks to the enduring connection between Jesus and Mary, even after his physical departure. How does this idea of an eternal spiritual bond challenge or enhance your understanding of relationships beyond this life?

9. Jesus acknowledges Mary's role in the spiritual evolution of humanity and the universe. How does this perspective of individual influence on a cosmic scale inspire you in your spiritual practices and sense of purpose?

10. In concluding his message, Jesus emphasizes that anything is possible if one keeps their light shining. How do you interpret this statement in the context of overcoming challenges and maintaining faith on your spiritual path?

Section 2:
Sarah's Spiritual Messages

Embracing New Beginnings

Dear Ones,

I send you my deepest love as I begin to share this message with you. With the recent eclipse, where the sky turned dark only to reveal the light once more, we were gifted a profound symbol of new beginnings. We all journey through these new beginnings because change is the nature of our soul's evolution. As human souls, you are ever-transforming, learning with each breath, and sometimes even within the very moments of your day.

As the solar eclipse unfolded, countless souls and immense energies converged to witness this cosmic event. The energy, the love, the spiritual connection—was truly astounding. I, along with the Sarah Collective, felt this surge of energy and was in awe of how the human collective unites to witness and celebrate such divine spectacles. It is in these moments that we recognize the magnitude of our connection and the birth of new beginnings.

Embrace this new beginning, refresh your vessel, and treat yourself with the love and reverence you deserve. Know your worth. Believe in yourself and in humanity, for we are all interconnected in this grand journey of learning and growth.

When you embrace a new beginning, it is as if you are presented with a blank canvas, a divine opportunity to create anew. Yet, be mindful of what you paint on this canvas; let it be something that nurtures your soul's spiritual journey. Reflect upon the imagery from the Bible, where God creates from clay, shaping, and molding. You too, as a reflection of the Divine, have the power to shape and create your own path, contributing to the collective, to the universe.

Some may wonder why suffering and challenges come into our lives. There is a saying, "bad things happen to good people," and it is often questioned. Let us reflect on the life of Jesus, a soul of pure love, who embodied the Divine in every way. One would think that such purity would be embraced, but instead, fear took root in the hearts of many. This fear arose because Jesus' teachings challenged the status quo, stirring what was comfortable, and this caused chaos.

It is crucial to understand that fear is the root of chaos. To dispel the chaos, we must face our fears and embrace the goodness that humanity holds. Love will always triumph. Love will always overcome. Jesus exemplified this. He was love, trust, and faith incarnate. He knew that the lessons he brought to Earth, and those he learned, were to be carried forward through generations, influencing not only Earth but the cosmos as well.

Remember, each day as you rise, ask yourself, "What am I learning?" Your lessons are not just for Earth but ripple out into the heavens, into the universe.

I, Sarah, leave you now with love and peace. Embrace who you truly are, for you are divine.

With blessings and light,

Sarah and the Collective

The Sacred Path of Creation

Dear Ones,

We come to you with messages of love and light, knowing that as you receive these words, you will feel the embrace of the divine. Today, we express our deep gratitude for welcoming us into your consciousness. This connection is a process.

For many of you, it can be challenging to surrender and allow spirit to guide you. This surrender extends into every aspect of your life. When you find yourself uncertain of your path, take a moment to sit in silence, to pray, and to commune with your spirit team, your angels, and your higher self. Yes, your higher self, for it is your truest guide on this spiritual journey. Your higher self knows what you need in this lifetime, for it is intimately connected to your soul's purpose.

This lifetime on Earth is a sacred opportunity for learning and growth. Earth is indeed a challenging place, and it is for this reason that we honor you. We celebrate your courage, your willingness to learn, and we are here to support you in every step. We, too, were once embodied, living lives with our own challenges and triumphs. The term 'common folk' resonates with us, for it reflects our shared humanity. We experienced the same struggles and joys, the ebb and flow of faith, just as you do.

We wish to bring forth the essence of Jesus, for in your current time on Earth, his teachings and presence are more relevant than ever. We speak of "time" as you understand it, though in truth, we exist beyond the confines of past, present, and future. The lessons of Jesus, though misunderstood by many during his life, continue to reverberate through the ages. His teachings were radical, challenging the norms of his time. Jesus, in his infinite love, swam against the tide, moving against the current to fulfill his divine purpose.

We, the collective of Sarah, knew Jesus, walked with him, and learned from his example of unconditional love. We are many, a sisterhood, united in purpose and spirit. Jesus treated us, and all women, as equals, acknowledging the divine spark within each of us. He understood that creation is not solely the work of man but is a reflection of the divine in all.

Sarah met Jesus in a small town, selling pottery she had crafted with her own hands. Each piece bore the imprint of her spirit, shaped with care and intention. When Jesus came to her, he did not simply admire her work; he inquired about her creative process, asking why she chose certain shapes, colors, and designs. She explained that each decision was guided by a deep sense of peace and authenticity, allowing her hands to flow freely, expressing her true self through her art.

Jesus encourages each of us to create, to use our hands, our minds, our hearts, to manifest our unique expressions of divinity. Do not judge what you create, for each creation is a reflection of your soul's journey. We are all different, each learning distinct lessons, yet we are united within the same divine collective. Imagine the world as a vast puzzle, each piece unique and essential. Together, these pieces form a complete picture, a harmonious whole.

At times, you may struggle to find where your piece fits. You may feel frustration when the path seems unclear, or when a puzzle piece does not align. In those moments, do not force it. Instead, set it aside with grace and trust that the right piece will find its place. Life is much like this puzzle; when a path feels wrong, when the piece does not fit, listen to your soul. It knows the way, and your spirit team is here to guide you, though the ultimate choice is yours to make. Your higher self, gifted with free will by God, is your truest guide.

Remember, beloved, you are a part of God, a reflection of the Divine. When you honor and worship God, you are also honoring the divine within yourself. We share these teachings with you to help you gather wisdom, like collecting precious gems in a jar, each representing a piece of divine knowledge. As you hold this jar, feel the presence of God, of Jesus, and know that you, too, are a part of this sacred container.

We leave you now with these lessons. Go forth and create your piece of the puzzle. Be true to yourself, for without your unique contribution, the collective is incomplete. Embrace your essence and move forward with love and purpose. Know that we, as a collective, are with you always.

With blessings and light,
Sarah and the Collective

Divine Oneness & Love

Dear Ones,

Jesus understood this profound truth—that the Divine Source, which some call God, is within each of us. He knew this intimately, but many sought truth outside themselves. Jesus endeavored to teach that the truth resides within; God is within. You are crafted from the very essence of God. Yet, many did not heed this message. It seems that humanity has not changed much over the ages. When I say "we," I include you in this time, for you are no different from those who walked the Earth alongside Jesus. Though the structures and communities around you may differ, and technology has advanced, the essence of humanity remains constant. We, too, lived close to nature, adapting to its rhythms and challenges, much like you do today.

This is why we come to you as messengers, for we once walked among you as human beings. The Bible recounts many characters, and if you look deeply, you will find that these figures are reflections of you. They felt and thought as you do, despite the differences in their surroundings.

These stories are not just tales from the past; they are mirrors of your own spiritual journey. We are all interconnected, all part of a universal collective. When people say, "We are one," it can seem like a difficult concept to grasp, but it is a fundamental truth. We are all one, united in spirit, learning and evolving together.

It is common for people to struggle with this concept, especially when they feel separate from others or witness behaviors they cannot comprehend. Yet, even in our differences, we are united. Each person is on their own path, learning their own lessons, and though their journey may seem far from yours, we are still pieces of the same grand puzzle. As humans, it is challenging to perceive this oneness because of our separate physical forms. But when we transition to the other side, we return to this unity, becoming part of the great light, where separateness no longer exists.

On the other side, there is a committee, not organized in the earthly sense with time and rules, but a gathering of souls from different galaxies and dimensions. This committee assists in the soul's learning and growth, helping each spirit fulfill its highest potential. And yes, Jesus is part of this collective, as is Gandhi, and many other enlightened souls. When you transition, you may see these figures in the form that resonates with you—Jesus, Gandhi, or another spiritual leader. But remember, all these forms are expressions of the same universal soul.

Earth is a place of diverse lessons, and religion is one of the many ways through which we learn. Some find their spiritual path early, others later in life, and some may change their beliefs along the way. Regardless of the path, all souls return to the same divine essence. Jesus taught that the way we treat each other on Earth should mirror the love and respect we show in the spiritual realms. We can create heaven on Earth when we support and heal one another, recognizing the divine in everyone.

Humans are social beings, meant to connect and uplift each other. Isolation can lead to darkness in the soul, but by embracing the love and light of others, we can nourish our spirits. In the spiritual realm, we are never alone, always surrounded by the love ot the collective. It is important to nurture your soul, to seek out positive energy, and to be in the warmth of the sun, which symbolizes divine love.

In our time, women often did the nurturing, offering love and care to others, even when they themselves were not nourished. Women gathered together, healing one another through their shared experiences and love. If you are a woman feeling alone, seek out a collective where you can share in this nurturing energy. Let the light within you shine, and in turn, you will illuminate others.

Your energy, your love, will ripple out to those in need, often without their conscious awareness. This is the power of divine love. As you move through life, be mindful of the energy you share with others. Send love through your words, actions, and presence. It will be felt, and it will uplift.

We leave you with this message today: go forth in love, be with others, nurture and love one another, and be open and vulnerable in your connections. The lessons you learn and share on Earth are powerful, transcending generations.

In times of difficulty, seek help, find that loving energy, and bask in the warmth of the sun. We surround you with love and light until we meet again.

With blessings and light,

Sarah and the Collective

Embracing the Unknown

Dear Ones,

When you embark on something new, it can feel unfamiliar, much like tasting a dish you've never tried before. Imagine someone presenting you with a beautifully prepared casserole, made with love, precision, and an array of spices. As you serve yourself a portion and take that first bite, your body recognizes it as nourishment, yet your mind hesitates, uncertain if you truly enjoy it or if you should continue.

But then you take another bite, and you begin to think, "This isn't so bad after all—better than the first." Your body and mind gradually adjust to the new flavors, and what was once unfamiliar becomes more palatable, even delightful. This is how we often experience new things in life. At first, there may be hesitation or discomfort, but as we embrace the experience, we adapt and often find unexpected joy.

So, when something new enters your life, welcome it with an open heart. It may not be instantly pleasing or easy, but it holds the potential to enhance your journey, not because your life needs improvement, but because every experience offers growth. You will meet new people along the way, people who may need to hear Sarah's message, or perhaps the messages of other collectives. But it all begins with a willingness to start, to take that first step into the unknown.

Know that you are not alone in this process. The collective will guide you, sending people and opportunities to support you in fulfilling our shared purpose. Trust the process, for we have a divine agenda, and we know the path we wish to walk with you.

With blessings and light,
Sarah and the Collective

Embracing Your Inner Light

Dear Ones,

I hope that today you are feeling the warmth of love surrounding you, and I pray that the message I bring to you will enrich your life and inspire deep reflection. We are deeply honored that you are taking the time to listen to us at this moment. And when I say "we," I speak of Sarah and the collective who are here to share this message with you.

The first thing we wish to remind you is that "you are light." When we speak of light, we are speaking of love, the highest form of energy. Each of you carries this divine light within, a sacred fire that resides in your soul. You have the power to choose how to use this light. You can shine it brightly for the good of humanity, to bring love and healing into the world, or you can choose to hide it away.

We are all here to learn and grow, and your light is a vital part of that journey. The more you share your light, the more you will feel the flow of love and energy returning to you. There may be times when your light seems to dim, weighed down by the challenges and emotions of earthly life. Know that this is part of your journey. Is is okay to feel these things deeply, for they are part of your learning and growth.

When your light feels dim, remember that it is only temporary. As you move through these experiences, your light will grow stronger and brighter, reflecting the lessons you have learned. How you navigate these moments of challenge will determine the brilliance of your light.

Sometimes, it is necessary to spend time alone to rekindle your light and nourish your soul. Solitude is a gift for the soul, a time to reconnect with your true essence. Even Jesus, who gave so much of himself to others, understood the need for solitude. He often retreated to quiet places to recharge, to reconnect with his divine purpose, and to keep his light shining brightly for all.

Jesus would walk beneath the stars, absorbing the energy of the universe, and replenishing his spirit. In today's world, distractions are abundant, pulling you away from your inner self. These distractions, while offering temporary relief, do not nourish your light. To truly replenish your energy, immerse yourself in nature. Walk in the woods, feel the energy of the trees, breathe deeply, and connect with the natural world around you. At night, when the sun has set, look up at the stars. Remember to look beyond yourself, to the vastness of the universe, and the divine energy that supports and protects you.

Your earthly vessel is designed to carry a certain amount of energy, but it is important to remember that you are connected to something much greater. When you feel your light dimming, take time to unplug from the devices and distractions of modern life. This different kind of energy can be relaxing, but it does not replace the deep, restorative energy that comes from within. Take time each day to be still, to be with yourself, to reconnect with your light. This practice will empower you, giving you the strength and clarity to continue your human journey with vigor and purpose. Empowerment is essential for your learning and growth. Keep learning, keep empowering yourself, and let your light shine brightly for all to see.

Know that you are never alone. When I say "we," I am speaking of God, of the ascended masters, of Master Jesus, of the angels, and of your loved ones who have crossed over. We are all here for you, watching over you, supporting your journey through these earthly experiences. Go forth in love and empowerment. We leave you now in love, light, and with the power to shine brightly.

With blessings and light,

Sarah and the Collective

Embrace Your Power

Dear Ones,

We are delighted that you are here today to receive our message. It is always uplifting to hear words of love and wisdom, and we hope this message will remind you of the divine love that flows within and through you. You are so important to this Earth. Your presence here is not by chance; you were born into this world because your soul is vital to its energy. Never doubt your significance, for you are a crucial part of this beautiful tapestry of life.

You chose the family and the circumstances you are in, for they offer the lessons your soul wished to learn in this lifetime. Do not be distracted by the outside noise, by the many stories that captivate the world. While they can be intriguing, remember that they are not necessarily your truth. These tales, often embellished as they are passed along, may entertain but are not meant to define you. Focus instead on your inner truth, the wisdom that resides within your heart.

In the time of Jesus, many were fascinated by material gains and the pursuit of power. Yet, Jesus taught that true power lies not in controlling others or the world around you, but in understanding and aligning with your higher self. Your higher self is always guiding you toward your truth, the truth that is more precious than any earthly control. Ask yourself why others seek to control you, and understand that it is because you have allowed it. But remember, you are not here to be controlled; you are here to learn, to grow, and to elevate the energy of the Earth.

Your words and thoughts are powerful tools of transformation. They can lift others up, or they can bring them down. Choose to see the divine in every person, and let your thoughts and words reflect that divine light. By doing so, you help others recognize their own light, raising their energy without exerting control, but simply by shining your own.

Jesus understood the power of words and thoughts. Around the campfire, he spoke with intention, knowing that his words carried the energy of transformation. Through meditation and mindfulness, you too can learn to master your thoughts, turning them towards love and positivity. This practice is like strengthening a muscle, and with time, you will find it easier to block negativity and cultivate thoughts that serve the greater good.

Remember, dear ones, *you are important.* This is why we, Sarah and the collective, come to speak with you. You are special to this Earth, and your presence here is a blessing. Focus on the present moment, and when worries arise, let them guide you toward positive action. Worry, when transformed into thoughtful reflection, can become a tool for change. Ask yourself, "What can I do to shift this energy? How can I bring forth thoughts of love and light?"

You are more powerful than you realize. God, the Divine, knows your worth, and your higher self knows it too. Treat your thoughts about yourself with care, for you are precious. You are light, you are love, and you are a powerful force on this Earth. This is the essence of what Jesus taught—to uplift not just those around him, but the very energy of the land.

Jesus would gather around the campfire, outside the towns, moving from north to south , east to west, consciously changing the energy around him. Each day, you have the same opportunity to change the energy that surrounds you. Follow your inner compass, and let it guide you to where your light is needed most.

We leave you now with love, reminding you of your specialness. Embrace and accept the beautiful light you bring to this Earth. Go forth in peace and love, knowing that you are cherished.

With blessings and light,

Sarah and the Collective

Awakening Your Spiritual Vision

Dear Ones,

Sarah and the collective are here with you once again, and we are grateful that you have chosen to listen to our message. Our hope is that each message fills you with energy, love, and a vision for a life rich in spiritual depth. In the fast-paced world of Earth, it is easy to forget the importance of having a vision, a spiritual guiding light that shapes your journey.

We encourage you to think of this vision as a movie playing in your mind. Just as you can replay scenes from a movie, so too can you visualize and immerse yourself in your spiritual vision. In the busyness of everyday life, many are absorbed in the latest technology, believing they are connected and have a clear vision. But true spiritual vision is not found in external distractions; it is found in the connection with your soul, with the Earth's energy, and with the heavens above.

Each person's vision is unique. When Jesus taught around the campfire, he guided us to leave behind our earthly worries and focus on the higher truths. This is not always easy, especially when confronted with suffering, but it is through this connection that we can help alleviate that suffering. Jesus showed us how to visualize, to connect deeply with the divine energy within and around us, to create a vision that transcends the physical realm.

To hold this vision, remember that we are all one. As we sat around the campfire, Jesus taught us that we are all streams of the same divine light, each carrying a piece of God's love. As we transition from this earthly realm to the next, we carry the lessons we've learned to the heavens and return with the divine energy, even if we do not consciously remember. This is why newborns are so deeply connected to the spiritual realm—they bring with them the fresh energy of the heavens and can see the souls of those around them.

When a baby is held by their parents, they see beyond the physical and feel the pure love of their souls. Even if their parents may not have fully embraced that love, the baby radiates divine energy, teaching and reminding them of love's true essence. Babies are powerful because they are untouched by the distractions of the world; they are pure, connected to the source.

We must learn to connect as they do, leaving behind our earthly problems to focus on our spiritual vision. It takes time and energy, but through patience and practice, you can remember why you are here and what your soul's purpose is. Visualize it, feel it deeply, and it will come to you. In the meantime, simply sending love energy out into the world is a powerful act. It is like a flower opening its petals, allowing your heart to open to the divine and the angels.

Jesus taught us the importance of opening our hearts, and as we sat around the campfire, I often visualized a flower blooming within me. As the flower opened, I felt the energy of the divine flowing in, connecting me to the angels and the heavens. Jesus explained that one day, these teachings would be written in a book, and each person who reads it would receive the message they need at that moment. This is why interpretations may differ, and it's important not to judge but to understand that each soul receives what it needs.

When you encounter someone who sees things differently, listen with love and compassion. Their message may offer you a new perspective, and by listening, you honor their journey. Remember, we are all part of a togetherness tribe, created by the Divine to support and learn from one another. When we come together, our vision becomes clearer, our understanding deeper, and the spiritual movie of our lives more vivid.

Sarah and the collective are sending you light and energy as we speak. We invite you to trust in your essence, to open the flower of your heart, and to see the vision that your soul needs to see. Go forth in peace, love, and divine connection.

With blessings and light,
Sarah and the Collective

Climbing the Mountain of Faith

Dear Ones,

We are grateful to be with you today, and we thank you for receiving our message. Today, we wish to speak about those moments when you feel uncertain, when you are lost and filled with anxiousness, unable to see which way to go. It is in these moments that faith becomes your guiding light.

Faith is like holding a dove in your hands and then releasing it, trusting that it will soar and return with the answers you seek. Visualize the dove flying off into the unknown and returning with a symbol of hope and life—a vine or a leaf—showing you that there is life, love, and guidance on the other side of your current experience.

When you are unsure of your path, when you cannot feel or see the way forward, lift your gaze to the spiritual realm, to the heavens. Offer a prayer, a mantra, something that elevates your energy to a higher vibration.

Faith is not something you can see with your eyes; it is something you feel within your heart. It is the knowing that the answers will come, even when the path is hidden from view.

Fear often arises when we cannot see what lies beyond the mountain in front of us. Jesus would often remind us around the campfire, "Climb the mountain, have faith in yourself, and trust that your faith will grow and empower you."

The journey may not be easy—you may stumble, and you may fall—but each lesson along the way strengthens you.

When you fall, feel the pain, acknowledge the difficulty, but then look up to the sky, to the sun, and draw strength from the divine light. When you are ready, rise again and continue your climb. Along the way, doubt may creep in, just as it did for Jesus when he retreated into solitude. He, too, faced moments of self-doubt, questioning whether his teachings would make a difference, whether anyone would listen. Yet, he kept walking, and as he climbed higher, the sun began to rise, casting its light and warmth over the mountain.

When you reach the summit, take a moment to look out over the horizon, to see the vastness of what lies before you. Sometimes, what you see may be overwhelming, too powerful to fully grasp in that moment. This is why there are many paths up the mountain, each offering different views and insights. The sun will guide you, empower you, and fill you with the peace and love of the Divine.

As you sit at the top of the mountain, meditate in silence. If no thoughts come, if you hear nothing, this is a blessing. It means you are absorbing the divine energy around you. Embrace the silence, for it is in this quietude that you connect most deeply with the divine.

When you feel ready, begin your descent. Carry with you the peace, tranquility, and insights you have received. Even if you cannot see everything clearly, trust that you have absorbed what you need, just as you trust in the unseen presence of faith. You may start to hear the gentle music of angels, feel the warmth of the sun within you, or sense your heart opening to divine love. These are all signs of your spiritual growth.

Remember, before you could experience this peace and love, you had to navigate through the chaos and fear. So, when you begin your day and feel lost or burdened, simply take one step at a time. Trust that peace will come if you allow it to.

Sarah and the collective are with you always. As we share this message, know that we feel your energy, even if you are not physically present with us. We close our physical eyes to better connect with your spiritual energy, for the soul's connection transcends the physical.

We leave you now with peace, with faith, and with love. Remember, you are never alone, and your journey is guided by the divine light within you.

With blessings and light,
Sarah and the Collective

Finding Hope in Everyday Miracles

Dear Ones,

How are you on this beautiful day, a day full of possibilities to create peace and to bring love into the world? We, Sarah and the collective, bid you peace and send our blessings. We hope that each day brings you fulfillment and the realization of your divine purpose.

Many people awaken each day and see what they choose to see. Will you see the sunshine, the new opportunities blossoming like spring with its green grass, blooming trees, and buzzing bees? Or will you see darkness, the gloom of a cloudy day that obscures the stars? Your thoughts shape your reality, so choose to see the sun, the possibilities, and the joy that each day offers. Every day is a gift, a miracle waiting to be embraced.

It is easy to feel alone, to feel unwell or weighed down by life's challenges. When you feel this way, it can be tempting to give in to dark thoughts, to lose sight of hope. But know this: your soul will feel lighter. Your spirit will lift when you choose to transform those into thoughts into positive ones. Seek the light, seek hope, for it always there, waiting to be found.

Many sought Jesus for hope. He was the beacon of light they needed in a world that felt heavy and devoid of joy. People walked with their heads down, burdened by their struggles, until Jesus came to them, bringing the hope they had lost. He traveled from town to town, spreading love, joy, and the miracles that rekindled the spark of life in those who had given up. People reached out to touch Jesus, not only for his healing power but for the beautiful energy that radiated from him.

Yet, remember that Jesus was human too. He had days when he felt the weight of the world, when he did not want to rise from his bed or leave his tent. But he knew the calling that urged him to continue, the need to bring hope to others. It is difficult to be joyful when you feel gloomy, but you have the power to rise above it. Find your empowerment in your solar plexus, and as you do, you will see the sun begin to peek over the horizon, bringing with it the promise of new possibilities.

As you embrace this hope, you will start to see the miracles around you. You will notice the energy that nature offers—the trees, the grass, the earth itself, all brimming with life and potential. Lay upon the earth and feel its grounding energy. This connection will restore your hope and uplift your spirit. And when you find this hope within yourself, you will naturally share it with others. Hope is contagious; as you uplift your own spirit, you help to uplift the collective energy of those around you.

We are all one, interconnected in this divine web of life. When one person sees hope, that light spreads and illuminates the path for others. This is when we can see clearly, make better decisions, and live in harmony with the greater good. You are part of the divine, an expression of God's love. Remember your divine nature and live in the present moment. Let go of the past, for it holds only lessons, and trust that the future will unfold as it should. Focus on who you are now, on the light and love you wish to share with the world.

Open your heart to the infinite possibilities and miracles that you can manifest. When your thoughts are pure and aligned with the divine, you will hear the whispers of the heavens guiding you. You are never alone; you are always surrounded by love and divine presence. We are all fragments of the divine, and as we come together, we form a greater whole. When you transition into the next realm, into the heavens, you will remember your true nature, and you will find peace.

But do not wait for that transition to experience peace. Do not believe that everything will be better only in the afterlife. Live your life fully as a human, for this is why you are here. Embrace the human experience, with all its challenges and triumphs. Feel deeply, learn, and grow, for there is plenty of time to dwell in the heavens. You are here to experience, to learn, and to grow in your spiritual journey.

You are powerful, more than you realize. Whatever comes to your door, know that you have the strength and empowerment to face it. Do not let challenges overcome you; instead, see them as opportunities to learn and evolve.

Shed your tears, for they are part of your healing. Let them flow, not just in sorrow but also in moments of hope and joy. Tears are a sign that you are alive, that you are feeling, and that your soul is engaged in this human experience.

We, Sarah and the collective, leave you now with peace, hope, and the energy you need to find your empowerment. We send you love and light, and we are honored to be with you on this journey.

With blessings and light,
Sarah and the Collective

Embrace Change

Dear Ones,

I hope the sunshine today fills your heart with joy. I, Sarah, along with the collective, bring you a message of inspiration and hope. Who among us doesn't need a reminder of our divine purpose, especially in the midst of life's changes?

As you build your cities and communities, as more souls come together to create something beautiful, progress unfolds. But with every step forward, change follows. You may wonder, what is changing? With every invention and advancement, there is an inevitable shift that can leave many feeling uncertain. It is natural to feel unsteady in times of change, as humans often find comfort in the familiar. Stability brings a sense of safety, but remember, you are here to learn, to grow, and to be flexible with the changes that come to Earth.

This does not mean abandoning your spirituality or forgetting who you are. On the contrary, it means embracing what is given to you and learning from it. Do not hide behind closed doors when faced with the unknown.

That is not what God intended. When Jesus walked the Earth, he knew he was there to shake things up, to bring about the change that humanity needed. He was aware of the challenges and the ultimate sacrifice he would make, but he knew it was necessary for the growth and evolution of mankind.

Jesus taught us that even in the midst of chaos, there is always love and hope. He lived his life as an example, showing that each day brings new opportunities to spread love and healing. As he walked from town to town, he did so with the knowledge that his path was uncertain, often met with resistance and anger. Yet, he continued, surrounded by those who loved him, understanding that change was essential for progress.

When changes come to your own community, know that they are part of the divine plan, meant to help you learn and grow. It is true that not everyone welcomes tribulations. Who among us would volunteer for pain and hardship? Yet, these experiences remind us of the good times, the joy, and they help us find our inner strength. You are here to experience the full spectrum of emotions—from happiness to sorrow, from excitement to peace.

God brings you what you need in the moment, whether it is the companionship of a beloved pet, the beauty of flowers, or the presence of a person who enters your life at just the right time. You have a divine plan, a map of lessons to learn and experiences to have. Your higher self is connected to God, and when you seek guidance, you are tapping into this divine connection. The universe is working with you because you are a precious part of something much greater.

Never doubt your worth. You are special, you are loved, and you are necessary for the divine tapestry of life. Even when you feel low, when others try to diminish your light, do not listen. Block those negative thoughts, and protect your energy. Know how to shield yourself from negativity, and embrace your true self. You are love, you are peace, you are joy. When faced with negativity from others, send them your loving energy, for they are the ones who need it most. Instead of reacting with anger, respond with compassion, and watch as the light within them begins to grow.

Life is full of changes, of people coming and going, and sometimes it is hard to let go. But think of a dandelion releasing its seeds into the wind, knowing that this is part of the natural order. Change is a constant in the universe, and it is good. Accept these changes, adjust your life accordingly, and trust that everything is unfolding as it should. Though the path may seem uncertain at first, know that there is a divine purpose behind every change.

Everything is written in the divine plan, guided by a higher power. You are never alone in these changes, for you are surrounded by the heavens, and within you lies the strength to find peace. We leave you now to adjust to the changes in your life, knowing that they are for your highest good, bringing peace and joy.

With blessings and light,

Sarah and the Collective

Embracing Life's Beauty

Dear Ones,

We wish to speak to you about the importance of joy in your life. Life is meant to be enjoyed, filled with love and joy. If you find yourself lacking in these, or surrounded by sadness, it is time to seek joy. We want you to be happy, to embrace life without fear. Soar like a bird in the sky. Just as a baby bird hatches from its egg and takes a leap of faith to learn how to fly, you too are meant to embrace your wings and experience the freedom and joy of life.

Although you are not built for physical flight, your energy is meant to soar. There is nothing more beautiful than seeing people sing and dance, coming together to worship in oneness with Jesus. He is one with you, and in your worship, you connect with this oneness. Feel the music, the choir, the community. They are not just singing; they are discovering their spirituality and joy. This brings peace into their lives.

When joy is absent, and fear or judgment take over, it diminishes the light in your heart. Fear leads to sadness. Remember, earthly judgment does not reflect the love and support from the heavens. We love you, we support you , and we bring you peace and joy, but you must open your heart to receive it. Spirituality can mean different things to different people, but it all comes from within. Your soul, your essence, is the light. This light is your joy, your spirit.

Do not seek spirituality outside of yourself. While learning and discussing different perspectives is beneficial, do not let judgment stifle your joy. Keep your heart open to endless possibilities. A hardened heart blocks out creativity and learning. Embrace the possibilities around you to find the joy within, allowing your light to shine brightly. Others will notice your radiance and be inspired by your joy.

Jesus walked great distances to share his message of peace and joy, to bring fulfillment to people's lives. Words carry power and frequency.

We leave you with this: Open your heart. Listen to the music. Worship with gratitude, not just to the heavens but also to yourself. Worship is a powerful word, but it does not have to be daunting. Find joy in your life, seek it, feel it, and let your light embrace it, so you can shine brightly. We bring you love, joy, and peace.

With love and blessings,

Sarah and the Collective

Navigating Life's Crossroads

Dear Ones,

We hope you are well during this time. Our messages are intended to bring you peace, joy, and love because we are here to spread love. Many people, when they hear messages channeled through us, think we are here to tell them what to do. This is not our purpose. Channeled messages are meant to bring you love, hope, peace, and the alchemy you need to be your true self. We convey different energies through our voices and our presence. Even though you are listening through this new technology, you are feeling the vibrations and energy in our message. This is what truly matters.

We do not tell you what to do because all the answers lie within you. You don't need anyone else to direct your path. Whatever decision you make is the correct one, even if the results are unexpected, because each choice opens new doors. One decision leads to another, creating a chain of experiences and opportunities for learning. Humans often overthink, analyzing every option to make the perfect decision, but sometimes this overthinking causes the opportunity to pass by.

I, Sarah, will explain further. Every opportunity, every event, has its own time and space. If you choose not to engage with a particular opportunity or energy, it will move on, and that's okay. You may not be ready for that path. The key is to listen to your heart. It's beneficial to find harmony with your surroundings, with Earth, and with your own energy. Meditation can help quiet the mind, slowing down your thoughts and allowing you to feel into the opportunity. How do you feel about it?

Finding mentors can also be helpful. If you decide on a direction, the universe will respond with the people and elements you need to continue on your journey. If your energy feels low and you aren't receiving answers, that might be your answer. Only you can decide.

We, the collective, want you to understand the immense power within you. This power not only helps you but also benefits the collective here on Earth. When faced with a decision, trust in your process. If you need to pray and reach out, remember that Jesus taught us to connect with the heavens. You have to ask for their assistance. If you want guidance from angels, they can help, though they won't tell you what to do. They can offer signs and guidance.

Many humans ask for signs and then become impatient, wanting immediate answers. Sometimes the universe takes time to respond because it doesn't operate within linear time. If you aren't listening, you might miss the symbols or signs we send. You may think you know what you want, but it's essential to stay open to the universe's response.

So, make sure you listen. If you need guidance, we are always here for you, but you must ask. If you have a deity or spiritual guide, ask them for help. They are there for you. We are here as one, ready to assist.

We leave you now with love, peace, and harmony. May you find the guidance you seek within yourself. Empower yourself to make any decisions along your journey. Go in peace, go in love.

With blessings and light,

Sarah and the Collective

Finding Peace

Dear Ones,

How are you on this beautiful day? Today is another opportunity to make peace and bring love to the world. We bid you peace.

I, Sarah, along with the collective, and we hope each day brings you fulfillment. Each morning, we have a choice: to see sunshine, new opportunities, the freshness of spring with green grass, blooming trees, and buzzing bees; or to see darkness, gloom, and a cloudy day where stars are hidden. Your thoughts are crucial. Try to see the sun, the possibilities, the joy in each day. Every day is a gift, a miracle if you choose to see it that way.

Many feel alone, unwell, and without hope, leading to dark thoughts. Changing these thoughts to more positive ones uplifts your energy and brings hope. Many sought Jesus for hope because he was a beacon of light in gloomy times. He walked from town to town to spread hope, love, and joy.

People wanted to touch Jesus not only for his healings but for the beautiful energy he radiated. Remember, Jesus was human too. He had gloomy days but knew the people needed hope, so he continued his mission.

It's difficult to be happy when feeling gloomy, but you can rise above it and find empowerment in your solar plexus. Once you find that empowerment, the sun starts peeking over the horizon, and you see hope, miracles, and the energy of nature. Lying in the grass and feeling the earth's energy can also give you hope. When you pick yourself up and see hope, you inspire others. Hope is contagious. We are all one, and when one person sees hope, we all see hope. This collective energy helps us make better decisions for our lives and others.

You are part of the divine, part of God, and here on earth for a reason. Live in the present, let go of the past, and trust the future will unravel itself. Focus on what you need and want, then let it go. Be the person you want to be now, showing others the true light and love. Open your heart to all possibilities and miracles that you can perform yourself. This is when you start hearing from the heavens, as pure thoughts connect you with divine guidance.

You are not alone. You are surrounded by divine pieces, and when you transition to the other world, you will be reminded of your origin and find peace. Don't wait for transition to bring better days. Live your life as a human, embracing human qualities and tribulations. Feel everything a human needs to live because there is plenty of time to be with the heavens.

You are here to learn and grow. You are very spiritual, and whatever comes your way, know you have the power to learn from it. It will not defeat you. You are in control, empowered. Shed tears when needed, in both gloom and hope, as they are part of your emotional journey.

I, Sarah, and the collective leave you in peace, giving you hope and the energy to find your empowerment. We send you love and are honored to be here with you today.

With blessings and light,

Sarah and the Collective

The Magic of Spiritual Alchemy

Dear Ones,

I hope you are doing well on this beautiful day. Make the best of it and shine your light. Be a beacon of light, like a lighthouse. We often forget what we need to bring into our lives. I love the word "alchemy." Many people think of alchemy as a magical soup made with special ingredients. This is true, but the alchemy I'm referring to involves the elements you need in your life, in your spirituality, to feel happy and connected to the heavens.

Each person's alchemy is unique. Think of three ingredients that you need in your life. These are the essential components that bring you joy, peace, love, and enlightenment. Some might need a sacred text to read daily, keeping them happy and enlightened. Others might require quiet meditation to stay connected to God and the source. Some may find solace in nature, feeling the energy of trees, watching birds, or observing the ripples on a lake.

For some, unconditional love is the key—love for themselves and others. How can we cultivate this love? It's not enough to say you want to love someone; you need to feel it deeply and infuse your energy with love. Imagine a balloon being filled with love. As it gets bigger, you might fear it will pop, but you can never have too much love. Let that balloon of love float into the sky, spreading your love to everyone. The universe reciprocates this love, as that is how it works.

In Jesus' time, around the campfire, he shared messages people needed to hear. Though his words were the same, each person took away a different meaning, tailored to what they needed at that moment. People gathered to discuss their interpretations, learning from each other without judgment. This highlights the importance of letting others interpret messages in their own way, as everyone's experiences and personalities shape their understanding.

When you share something that fills you with divine energy, allow others to receive it in their own way. Their interpretation is their truth, and it's valid. During biblical times, people needed to hear about love because negativity was prevalent. They embraced Jesus' message because it radiated love and divine energy. He spoke to their souls, not just their minds, which is why people were drawn to his presence.

You, too, can radiate love. Even when faced with negativity, continue to love unconditionally. Your love and energy can transform others. Remember, you are mystical and magical, a part of the divine. Don't forget this.

Now, consider what three elements you want to include in your daily spiritual practice. These elements will change over time, and that's okay. Feel free to adjust your alchemy as needed. Thank the ingredients that have served you well and replace them with new ones as you grow.

I, Sarah, and the collective, leave you with love, peace, and magic. Remember the magic within you and the magical elements your soul possesses.

With blessings and light,

Sarah and the Collective

Messages from Heaven

Dear Ones,

Today unfolds like a new blossom, inviting the warmth of the sun and the gentle embrace of peace and love. Sarah and the collective draw near to speak with you about the sacred nature of spiritual events. You may wonder, "What is a spiritual event?" It is a gift from the heavens, arriving unexpectedly, touching your soul with an awe-inspiring moment of divine clarity.

Why do these spiritual events occur? From where do they arise? Many find themselves unsure of how to react when they witness something spiritual or receive a message they desperately needed to hear. These encounters may overwhelm you, filling you with a sense of wonder. And this is indeed marvelous. The heavens send you these spiritual events as gentle reminders of the spiritual world's presence, assuring you that you are never alone. These moments can be as fleeting as a butterfly's flight—gracing your awareness for just an instant before it vanishes. Yet, in that moment, the heavens whisper,

"Hello."

Who are these heavenly beings reaching out to you? They may be your loved ones who have crossed over, offering their love and support. They could be your spiritual guides, walking alongside you, affirming, "Well done. We are here with you, loving you." Or perhaps it is your higher self, watching from above, bestowing you with strength and empowerment. It may even be the Divine, the Source of All, embracing you with warmth, love, and support, surrounding you with all that you need in this moment. When these heavenly occurences happen, receive them with gratitude, for they are precisely what you needed at that time.

Do not be afraid to share your heavenly experiences. Sometimes, your experience, even if you do not fully understand it, can be a guiding light for others. They may resonate with it in ways you cannot foresee, for spiritual energy and vibration are unique to each soul. By witnessing these sacred events, you may unknowingly provide comfort and insight to someone who is yearning for it.

Many hesitate to share their spiritual encounters, fearing judgment from others. But remember, do the angels concern themselves with how they are perceived when they visit? Miracles unfold around us every day, reminding us that we dwell in a sacred space, surrounded by divine presence. These miracles are invitations to open our hearts to the reality of heaven, here and now.

When Jesus ascended into the heavens, He returned to reveal the eternal nature of life. His transformed, heavenly body was unrecognized by even those who knew him best. Likewise, when loved ones or angels visit, they may take on forms that are familiar yet altered, reflecting their happiest or most peaceful moments. Often, they will appear as you remember them, but sometimes your memory may falter, just as the disciples did not recognize Jesus.

In dreams, when your conscious mind is at rest, your loved ones may visit, bringing peace and comfort. Do not doubt these encounters. Embrace them, for they are real and come to you for a reason, at the precise moment when you need them most. These heavenly events happen with purpose, each one a divine appointment.

Jesus may come to you in a form that differs from the traditional depictions in scripture or church teachings. He may appear in a way that feels familiar and comforting to you, for he desires to connect with you in love and understanding. If his appearance is unexpected, know that he does so because he loves you and seeks to bridge the gap between heaven and earth.

In the times when we gathered around the campfire, Sarah and the collective could see the light within Jesus, a light so profound that his face would shift and change, revealing different faces to each of us. We each saw something unique, reflecting our own hearts' needs. So too, when you encounter a spiritual being and their appearance shifts, know that this is done for your benefit, offering you what your soul requires in that moment.

Miracles and visits from the divine often come during times of chaos, for it is then that we need them most. As Sarah and the collective take their leave, remember that if you desire to connect with a loved one or spiritual guide, you can set the intention and pray. The heavenly bodies are intricately woven into the fabric of the earth, and they will respond, for we are all one. The veil between realms is thin, and heaven is all around you.

We leave you now in peace and love, trusting that you will find solace in this message.

With blessings and light,

Sarah and the Collective

Embracing the Light

Dear Ones,

We greet you on another beautiful day, hoping that the sun's light is shining upon you and that your heart is filled with warmth. Today, Sarah and the collective wish to speak with you about the nature of fear in our lives.

Fear is not something we are born with; it is learned from the energies and behaviors of those around us. We absorb the fear of others, and it takes root within us, growing in moments when we feel vulnerable or uncertain. Fear stands in opposition to love and faith, and when we dwell in fear, we invite negative energies to multiply within us.

Imagine a flower blooming in a sunlit field, its petals reaching out to the light. But if this flower becomes fearful—worried that the sun might not shine tomorrow or that rain might never come again—it begins to wither. The petals fall, and the vibrant life it once radiated fades. Fear is like a shadow that dims the light within us, spreading like a disease that turns the beauty of life into darkness.

While fear can serve a purpose in protecting us from harm, it can also paralyze us, turning potential danger into overwhelming terror. This fear can linger, imprinting itself on places and spaces, leading to a sense of heaviness or negativity that others can feel. Sometimes, we misinterpret this energy as something sinister when, in truth, it is the residue of fear and pain left behind by others.

It is important to remember that even those who carry negative energy are still a part of the whole—they are part of us. Instead of rejecting them, we can send them light and prayers, offering them the calm and warmth of love. They have the free will to release their fear and seek the light, but they may not know where to find it unless they encounter someone who embodies it. You can be that light, a beacon that inspires others to choose love over fear.

In today's world, it is easy to be consumed by fear, especially when people expose themselves to the constant stream of negativity that can come through media and news. The simplest solution is to distance yourself from these sources of fear, but even more powerful is to transform that fear into light. When you hear or see something that stirs fear within you, use that moment to pray and send positive energy into the world. Remember, you are in control of how you receive and respond to this information.

Around the campfires, Jesus spoke of love, peace, and truth. Yet, many were fearful, burdened by past experiences that made it difficult to trust in his words. Some even became angry, unable to comprehend the purity of his light because it shone so brightly in contrast to their own inner darkness. This is why some fear spirituality —they see the light in others and it stirs discomfort within them because it challenges their own shadows.

You must remember that fear and judgment are not the paths to growth. Instead, call to embody love, truth, and harmony. Like flowers, you bloom in the presence of light and wither in darkness. Yet, you have free will—some may choose to hold onto fear as part of their earthly lessons. They may seek to understand what fear is, for in the realm of the divine, there is no fear, only truth, love, and radiant energy.

When you encounter someone who is gripped by fear or has turned that fear into anger, know that they are on their own journey of learning. Show them a different way—let your light shine so that they can see the possibility of love and faith.

They may choose to hold onto their fear, and if they do, that is their free will. You must honor their path while protecting your own light. If their negativity begins to affect you, it is wise to step away, preserving your energy and well-being.

Surround yourself with love and light, as the Divine Source, Jesus, and the heavens wish for you. This is your path, your choice in this lifetime. And as you walk this path, know that you are never alone.

We leave you now, wrapped in love, peace, truth, and most of all, harmony.

With blessings and light,

Sarah and the Collective

Finding Strength in Unity

Dear Ones,

Greetings on this beautiful and sunlit day. Sarah and the collective gather here with you to share a message of inspiration and upliftment. In times when your mind is overflowing with thoughts, when you find yourself overthinking and trying to carry the weight of the world alone, remember this: it is okay to seek help. Sometimes, our ego convinces us that we must be strong and courageous, that we must do everything on our own. But there is great wisdom in reaching out to others.

You are not alone on this journey; you are surrounded by a collective, a community of souls with shared experiences and common visions. These are your soul companions, here to support and guide you. When you try to navigate life's challenges in isolation, it is easy to feel lost, unsure of which direction to take. But when you open your heart to the heavens and ask for guidance, help will come in the form of those around you, offering the wisdom and support you need.

When someone approaches you with advice or guidance, let go of your ego and be open to receiving their words. It's okay to be wrong to change your perspective—that's how we learn and grow. Frustration and anger may arise, but remember, these emotions are part of your process, and those who offer you help do so out of love. They may set you on a path that, though it may not be what you wanted or expected, is exactly where you need to go.

Consider the image of a dog, free to roam the fields, delighting in the scents and sights of the world. Yet, as hunger sets in, the dog realizes that surviving alone is not as easy as it seemed. Guided by its instincts, the dog follows a scent to a home where a little girl offers it food and love. Though the dog initially sought freedom, it finds something deeper in the love and companionship of the girl. In choosing to stay with her, the dog discovers a new kind of freedom— one that is nourished by connection and care. Even after the dog transitions to the spirit realm, it continues to watch over the girl, their bond enduring through lifetimes.

Similarly, in the time of Jesus, around the campfires, He spoke of the love, peace, and truth that transcend all fear. Though many feared the unknown, angered by what they did not understand, Jesus remained a beacon of light. His presence and teachings continue to guide us, even after his earthly departure. His energy is always with us, manifesting in ways that we can recognize and connect with, bringing love into our hearts.

When you hear birds singing outside your window, know that they are messengers of the divine, their voices carrying the energy of angels. They sing to remind you of the sacred presence around you. Listen closely, for their song may carry messages from Jesus, from your loved ones, or from the heavens themselves. And when things do not go as planned, remember that the heavens may send you exactly what you need at that moment, even if it is not what you wanted.

We are all interconnected, part of the same divine tapestry, helping each other ascend to higher vibrations, to become more aligned with our true selves. When you encounter someone who speaks the words you need to hear, recognize it as a moment of divine guidance. There is no need for anger or resistance—everything unfolds as it is meant to.

Take a deep breath, allowing it to raise your energy and free your spirit. Your light, like a candle, will sometimes flicker low and other times burn brightly. Embrace these fluctuations, for they are part of your journey. And when you need help, pray and set the intention for guidance. Remember, humans are not meant to walk this path alone.

We leave you now with love, sending you flowers from heaven. When you catch the scent of flowers with no bloom in sight, it is an angel or a loved one saying hello. When you hear the birds sing, know that it is also a heavenly greeting. Embrace these signs, for they are gentle reminders of the divine love that surrounds you always.

May you walk your spiritual path with grace, knowing that you are supported, loved, and never alone.

With peace and love,

Sarah and the Collective

Navigating Life with Truth & Energy

Dear Ones,

Good day to you all. We, Sarah and the collective, are grateful for your presence and your willingness to listen. Today, we wish to share with you the profound connection between truth and energy. You may wonder why we speak of truth and energy together, and it is because they are inseparable. When you live in your truth, you align with your highest energy.

Finding your truth and self-worth, discovering who you truly are, can be a challenging journey. The ego often questions and doubts, much like a stern parent influenced by society's expectations. Society, in different times and places, dictates how we should think, act, and feel. These external pressures can obscure our true selves, making it difficult to live authentically.

Throughout history, many have been persecuted for following their truth, facing dire consequences for defying societal norms. This fear can cause us to hide our true selves, to protect our families and ourselves from harm. But even in the face of earthly challenges, we are

are called to seek our truth, to live in the light of our soul's essence.

You may ask, "How do I find my truth, my true energy, whenovershadowed by the world's problems?" Jesus, around the campfire, shared with us the importance of silence and meditation in this quest. Sitting in silence, clearing your mind of the ego's chatter, is where you will encounter your true self.

It is through meditation and breath work that you cleanse your thoughts and connect with the core of your being. Breath is the bridge between your body and soul, clearing your energy and grounding you in peace.

When I struggled to quiet my mind, Jesus would sit with me, guiding me through breathing exercises. This practice centered me, allowing me to find peace and accept myself more fully, free from the grip of fear. If fear arises during your meditation, acknowledge it gently. Say to it, "I see you, but I do not need you now. I am my own soul, and I know what I need." As you recognize your light and speak your truth, your heart will open, revealing your true essence.

Your energy will become more vibrant as you embrace your truth. You will know you are on the right spiritual path when your energy feels light and uplifting. Remember, it is normal to have moments of low energy—this is part of the human experience. However, living in your truth will help you navigate these difficult times with grace and resilience.

When you look into the mirror, you may begin to see yourself differently. As you align with your truth and energy, your reflection may change, revealing a deeper, more authentic version of yourself. You may even catch glimpses of your past lives, as your face subtly morphs, showing you the many forms your soul has taken. This should not be frightening; it is a beautiful reminder of your soul's eternal journey.

Our past lives influence our reactions to present situations, often pushing us to make different choices to alter the outcomes. This is part of your growth—choosing differently to see where your story leads. As your light shines brighter, others will be drawn to you, wanting to be part of your journey. However, some may be repelled by your light, and that is okay. It is simply means you are on different frequencies.

When this happens, send love to those who are not yet ready to join you on your path. It is not a rejection of them, but an honoring of where you both are. You are here to live your truth, and they are on their own journey of discovery.

In the days when I would go into town to share Jesus' teachings, I often encountered resistance. People were not always ready to hear the truth, and their fear would manifest as anger or avoidance. I learned to see this with compassion, understanding that they were simply not ready to receive the light. I sent them love and left them to find their way, knowing they could join us at the campfire when they were ready.

As you find your energy of truth, you may also find new truths revealed to you—truths that were hidden but are now ready to be discovered. This is a joyous experience, a celebration of the unfolding of your soul. Embrace these revelations, for in celebrating yourself, you also celebrate the collective, of which you are an integral part.

We leave you now, encouraging you to seek your truth, to sit with your soul in silence, and to practice the breath work that clears your mind and elevates your energy. Your energy is always with you, waiting for you to engage with it, to explore and expand it.

Go forth on your path with love, peace, and self-harmony.

With blessings and light,
Sarah and the Collective

The Healing Power of Sunlight & Stars

Dear Ones,

Greetings to you on this marvelous day. We, Sarah and the collective, come to share a message about the profound significance of sunshine and light in your lives.

How often, when you are feeling low and your energy is depleted, do you retreat indoors, away from the sunlight and the warmth of others' light? While this may seem like a temporary refuge, day after day of avoiding the sun can cause the light within you to dim as well. Sunshine is more than just a source of nutrients for your body —it is a wellspring of joy and warmth for your soul. It nourishes your spirit, allowing it to grow and flourish.

The sun is, indeed, a star. And just as the sun lights up your days, the stars light up your nights, reminding you that life continues beyond our Earth, extending into other universes, into infinity. When you look up at the stars, imagine that there is someone in another universe also gazing at those same stars. In that moment, your souls connect across the vastness of space, sharing a silent bond, feeling eachother's energy, even without knowing one another's form.

I invite you to embrace this connection. Go outside, lie down on the grass, feel the energy of Mother Earth beneath you, and gaze up at a star. Focus on that one star and allow your energy to merge with it. See what kind of energy you receive in return. If you are feeling unwell, looking up at the stars can enlighten your soul, reminding you of the boundless light that exists even in the darkest night.

During the day, if your spirits are low and you find yourself reluctant to step into the sun, take just a few moments to sit outside. Let the sun's rays touch your skin, filling you with warmth and energy. In this meditative state, you are like a battery, recharging with the light and warmth that the sun provides. As you sit in this light, set an intention or offer a prayer. Know that your energy is being lifted to the heavens, connecting with the divine and the energy surrounding you.

When God created this Earth, He gave us the sun to light our days, ensuring that we would not live in darkness. The rising sun marks the beginning of each new day—a fresh start, a new opportunity. When you step outside before dawn and watch the sun rise, listen to the insects and the birds. They, too, know that a new day has begun, a day full of potential and possibility.

If you find yourself facing a dark and difficult day, remember that the next day may be filled with sunshine. Each day is different, and your perspective can transform the way you experience it. If you feel the need for more light, step outside into nature. Hug a tree, listen to the birds, immerse yourself in the light. Just as your phone needs to be recharged to function, so too does your soul need the light to thrive.

Take time away from your work, step outside, walk on the grass, and surround yourself with trees. This simple act will revitalize your body, mind, and spirit, allowing you to return to your tasks with renewed imagination and clarity. The light you absorb will uplift your energy, helping your thoughts to flow more freely, your ideas to blossom.

Even in the darkness of night, remember that there is always light. The stars above, even in their faint glow, remind us that light is never truly absent. So, I leave you with this thought: ensure that you step outside and recharge yourself in the light. Do not remain indoors too long, for that is where sadness and depression can take hold. Each day is a new beginning. Rise early, witness the sunrise, and let every miracle of the new day unfold before you. Listen to the birds— they are alive, celebrating the gift of life, and so should you.

Shine your light brightly so that your body, mind, and soul remain healthy, enabling you to continue on your spiritual journey. This is the purpose of your existence.

I, Sarah, leave you now with love. May you find your truth and your spiritual wisdom.

With light and blessings,

Sarah and the Collective

Section 3:

The Alchemy of Divine Essence

Truth, Wisdom & Love

The Alchemy of Divine Essence

S arah's channeled messages emphasize the timeless teachings of Jesus, shared around the sacred campfires, where the profound alchemy of truth, wisdom, and love was illuminated. These teachings, known as Christ Consciousness, transcend any particular religion or belief system, representing a universal concept that embodies the highest level of spiritual awakening one can attain.

Christ Consciousness is the realization of our true nature as divine beings, intimately connected to the Source of all creation. Those who embrace this consciousness live in a state of unity with God, transcending the limitations of the ego and the material world, and embodying the divine presence in every aspect of their lives.

Spiritual Truth, Wisdom, and Love

Spiritual Truth is the foundation upon which all spiritual growth is built. It is the eternal and unchanging reality that transcends the illusions of the material world. For those who seek a deeper connection with the divine, embracing spiritual truth means aligning with the teachings of Jesus, who embodied truth in its purest form. He taught that the truth would set us free, liberating us from the chains of ignorance and fear. In our quest for spiritual truth, we learn to see beyond appearances, recognize the divine presence within ourselves and others, and live in a way that honors this sacred truth.

The call to Know thyself serves as a powerful reminder of the importance of recognizing our spiritual truth. By knowing our true essence beyond the ego or societal roles, we understand our essence beyond the ego or societal roles, we understand our soul's purpose and live authentically.

Spiritual Truth reveals that we are all interconnected, that we all make mistakes as part of our human journey, and that holding onto anger or resentment only separates us from this truth. Recognizing the oneness of all beings and the divine spark within each person, forgiveness naturally extends from this truth. In forgiving others, we also free ourselves, beginning the healing process that comes from acknowledging and releasing false beliefs, limiting patterns, and the illusions that block our connection to the divine.

Spiritual seekers must master their own spiritual truth to fully receive and understand spiritual wisdom from the higher realms.

Ten Ways to Deepen Your Spiritual Truth

1. *Meditation*: Spend time in meditation to quiet the mind and connect with your inner self. Meditation allows you to go beyond surface thoughts and tap into deeper levels of consciousness where spiritual truth resides.

2. *Journaling*: Regularly reflect on your thoughts, actions, and beliefs. Journaling can be a powerful tool for understanding your motivations, uncovering hidden truths, and aligning more closely with your spiritual path.

3. *Study Sacred Texts & Teachings*: Delve into sacred writings from your spiritual tradition or explore the teachings of enlightened beings like Jesus, Buddha, or other spiritual leaders. Contemplate the deeper meanings behind these teachings and how they apply to your life.

4. *Practice Mindfulness*: Cultivate mindfulness in your daily activities. Being fully present in the moment helps you recognize the divine in everyday life and see things as they truly are, beyond illusions and distractions.

5. *Connect with Nature*: Nature reveals spiritual truths through its beauty, simplicity, and interconnectedness. Spend time in natural settings to connect with the earth and experience the oneness of all creation. Grounding exercises, such as walking barefoot on the earth, can also help you connect with your body and the earth's energy, fostering a deeper sense of spiritual truth.

6. *Practice Compassion & Forgiveness*: Actively practice compassion toward yourself and others. Compassion dissolves barriers, leading to a greater understanding of spiritual truth. Forgiveness is a powerful tool for releasing negative energy and aligning with spiritual truth. Letting go of grudges and resentment opens your heart to greater love and truth.

7. *Embrace Silence & Solitude*: Regular periods of silence allow you to hear the still, small voice within, where spiritual truth often reveals itself. Silence helps you disconnect from the noise of the world and tune in to the divine.

8. *Practice Gratitude:* Regularly expressing gratitude shifts your focus to the positive aspects of life and fosters a deeper connection with the divine. Gratitude helps you recognize the spiritual truths present in everyday experiences.

9. *Serve Others:* Serving others with love and compassion deepens your understanding of interconnectedness and spiritual truth. Through service, you experience the joy of giving and the spiritual truth of unity with all beings.

10. *Listen to Your Intuition:* Your intuition is a direct link to spiritual truth. Learn to trust and follow your inner voice, even when it defies logic or external expectations.

Spiritual Wisdom is the understanding and application of spiritual truth in our daily lives. While truth provides the foundation, wisdom is the guiding light that helps us navigate the complexities of life with discernment and grace. Jesus, as the embodiment of divine wisdom, showed us how to live in alignment with God's will, making choices that reflect love, compassion, and justice. Spiritual wisdom enables us to see the interconnectedness of all things, to make decisions that uplift ourselves and others, and to walk a path that leads to spiritual fulfillment.

When we integrate forgiveness into our lives, we expand our spiritual wisdom and gain deeper insights into ourselves and others. Spiritual forgiveness involves letting go of the emotional and energetic bonds that keep us attached to resentment, anger, or hurt, freeing us for greater healing and growth.

Forgiveness requires the discernment and deep understanding that come with spiritual wisdom. It involves seeing beyond the surface of hurtful actions to recognize the underlying causes, often rooted in pain, ignorance, or fear. Wisdom guides us to forgive, knowing that it heals not only the person who forgives but also the broader spiritual ecosystem. It teaches us that forgiveness is not about condoning wrongdoing but about releasing the burden of anger and opening the heart to healing.

Through wisdom, we learn to approach healing with patience, compassion, and a deep awareness of what is truly needed for our highest good.

Ten Ways to Deepen Your Spiritual Wisdom

1. *Study Sacred Texts*: Delve into sacred texts from your spiritual tradition, such as the Bible, Bhagavad Gita, Quran, Torah, or other spiritual writings. Reflect on the deeper meanings and how they apply to your life.

2. *Seek Guidance from Teachers & Mentors*: A spiritual teacher or mentor can provide personalized guidance, share their wisdom, and help you navigate your spiritual journey. Participate in spiritual lectures, workshops, retreats, and seminars led by knowledgeable teachers to gain deeper insights into spiritual topics.

3. *Engage in Regular Meditation & Prayer*: Regular prayer opens channels of communication with the divine, fostering a deeper connection and understanding of spiritual knowledge. Meditation helps you connect with your inner self and the divine, allowing spiritual knowledge to emerge from within. Different forms of meditation can enhance your understanding of spiritual concepts.

4. *Join Study Groups or Spiritual Communities*: Join a study group focused on spiritual texts or topics. Discussing and sharing insights with others can deepen your understanding and provide new perspectives. Being part of a spiritual community provides support, shared experiences, and collective learning, enriching your spiritual knowledge.

5. *Practice Self-Reflection & Journaling*: Take time to reflect on spiritual teachings and how they relate to your life. Contemplate their meanings and how you can apply them.

6. *Explore Different Spiritual Practices & Rituals*: Explore different spiritual practices such as yoga, fasting, chanting, or breathwork. These practices can deepen your experiential knowledge of spirituality. Engage in spiritual rituals that resonate with you, such as lighting candles, using incense, or creating an altar. Rituals can help anchor spiritual knowledge in daily life.

7. *Seek Inner Guidance & Intuition*: Your intuition and inner guidance can be powerful sources of spiritual knowledge. Learn to listen to and trust this inner voice. Regularly ask for divine guidance in your studies and spiritual practices, and remain open to the wisdom that comes through.

8. *Ponder Deep Questions*: Reflect on life's big questions, such as the nature of existence, the purpose of life, and the meaning of suffering. Contemplating these mysteries can lead to profound spiritual insights.

9. *Engage with Nature*: Nature is a profound teacher of spiritual truths. Spend time outdoors, observe the natural world, and reflect on the lessons it offers. Grounding exercises, like walking barefoot on the earth, help connect you with the earth's energy and enhance your spiritual awareness.

10. *Cultivate a Disciplined Spiritual Routine:* Consistency is key to deepening spiritual knowledge. Establish a daily routine that includes prayer, meditation, study, and reflection.

Spiritual Love

Spiritual Love is the highest expression of spiritual truth and wisdom. Jesus' teachings are rooted in love—unconditional, boundless, and transformative. Love is the force that heals, unites, and elevates the soul. It is through love that we fully embody spiritual truth and wisdom, as it compels us to act with kindness, forgiveness, and empathy. Love is not merely an emotion but a state of being that reflects our true nature and our connection to the divine. Jesus taught that love is the greatest commandment, the essence of all spiritual practice, and the path to eternal life.

At its core, forgiveness, is an act of spiritual love. It is the embodiment of unconditional love, central to Christ Consciousness. Forgiveness flows naturally from a heart filled with love, understanding that love transcends all grievances and is expansive enough to encompass even those who have wronged us. In this sense, forgiveness is both a product of love and a path back to it, restoring harmony and unity in relationships and within the self. Love heals by dissolving fear, anger, and resentment, replacing them with forgiveness, compassion, and acceptance. When we open ourselves to divine love, we allow its healing power to flow through us, healing not only our own wounds but also extending healing to others.

Love is the essence of all true healing, whether it occurs on a physical, emotional, or spiritual level.

Twelve Ways to Deepen Your Spiritual Love

1. *Practice Unconditional Love*: Make a conscious effort to love others regardless of their actions, beliefs, or differences. This mirrors the divine love that is given freely and without judgment. Extend your love beyond just those close to you, to all living beings, recognizing the divine spark within everyone.

2. *Cultivate Compassion*: Put yourself in the shoes of others, understanding their struggles, pains, and joys. Compassion helps bridge the gap between self and others, deepening spiritual love.

3. *Engage in Forgiveness*: Let go of grudges, resentment, and anger. Forgiveness frees the heart and allows love to flow more abundantly. It is a powerful act of love that heals both the giver and the receiver. Self-forgiveness is also crucial for deepening spiritual love. Recognize your own imperfections and embrace yourself with compassion and understanding.

4. *Meditate on Love*: Practice meditations focused on love, such as loving-kindness (Metta) meditation. In these meditations, you visualize sending love to yourself, others, and all beings. Meditate on the heart chakra, the energy center associated with love and compassion. Visualizing this area filled with light can help expand your capacity for love.

5. *Express Gratitude*: Regularly express gratitude for the love in your life, the people who care for you, and the beauty of the world. Gratitude amplifies love by focusing on the positive aspects of life. Offer gratitude to the divine or higher power for the love and support you receive, deepening your connection to spiritual love.

6. *Serve Others with Love*: Serve others without expecting anything in return. Acts of service rooted in love connect you to the divine and deepen your experience of spiritual love.

7. *Live Mindfully*: Recognize the beauty and love in each moment, whether in nature, relationships, or daily activities. This awareness helps cultivate spiritual love.

8. *Practice Self-Love:* Take care of your physical, emotional, and spiritual well-being. Self-love is the foundation for loving others, as it allows you to give from a place of fullness.

9. *Surround Yourself with Loving Energy:* Fill your living space with symbols of love, such as inspiring quotes, images, or objects that remind you of love. This creates an atmosphere that nurtures spiritual love. Spend time with people who embody love and positivity. Their energy will inspire and uplift you, deepening your own experience of love.

10. *Reflect on the Teachings of Love:* Delve into spiritual texts that focus on love, such as the teachings of Jesus, the Bhagavad Gita, or the teachings of Buddha. Reflect on how you can apply these teachings in your life. Read or listen to the teachings of spiritual leaders known for their embodiment of love, such as Mother Teresa, the Dalai Lama, or Rumi.

11. *Embrace Love's Challenges:* When faced with difficult situations or people, choose love over anger, resentment, or fear. These challenges are opportunities to deepen your spiritual love.

12. *Strengthen Your Connection with the Divine:* Allow yourself to surrender to the love of the divine, trusting that you are supported and guided by a higher power. This trust opens your heart to deeper levels of love. Regular prayer also helps deepen your connection to the divine source of love. Ask for guidance in embodying and expressing love more fully in your life.

For those searching for spiritual truth, wisdom, and love, these elements are not separate but interconnected aspects of the same divine alchemy. They are the keys to unlocking a deeper understanding of Jesus' teachings and embodying Christ Consciousness in our lives. By seeking truth, cultivating wisdom, and living in love, we transform ourselves and the world around us, fulfilling the spiritual purpose that Jesus came to reveal.

Remember....Christ Consciousness can also be understood as Divine Awareness, Universal Love, or God Consciousness, reflecting a state of Spiritual Enlightenment and connection with the Higher Self. It embodies Sacred Awareness and Cosmic Consciousness, emphasizing a deep sense of Oneness with God, Divine Wisdom, and Holy Awareness. This state invites one to experience Universal Unity, Divine Light, and Spiritual Unity, rooted in Sacred Truth and the realization of Unity Consciousness.

Section 4:

A Letter to Sarah

Your Spiritual Reflections

Dear Sarah:
Your Sacred Connection

How to Write Your Letter

As you journey through the pages of this story, you are invited to deepen your connection with Sarah and her teachings. This section is a sacred space where you can share your thoughts, ask questions, and express your feelings directly to Sarah. Writing a letter to Sarah is an opportunity to reflect on your spiritual path, seek guidance, or simply connect with the love and wisdom she offers.

Express Your Thoughts and Feelings: Use this space to communicate openly with Sarah. You may want to share personal reflections, express gratitude, or explore any challenges you're facing on your spiritual journey.

Ask for Guidance or Support: If there's an area in your life where you feel uncertain or in need of guidance, consider asking Sarah for her spiritual insight. This could be related to your relationships, personal growth, or your connection to the divine.

Set Intentions or Offer Prayers: You might wish to set intentions for your spiritual development or offer prayers for yourself or others. This is a time to articulate your hopes and desires, trusting in the alchemy of Truth, Wisdom, and Love to support you.

Write from the Heart: There's no right or wrong way to write this letter. Whether it's a few simple sentences or a lengthy reflection, what matters is that it comes from your heart.

Where Do I Send the Letter?

After writing your letter, you can send it by e-mail to Michelle Henderson at:

michelle@michellethechanneler.com

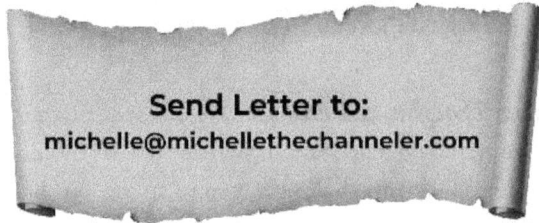

Send Letter to:
michelle@michellethechanneler.com

www.ingramcontent.com/pod-product-compliance
Lightning Source LLC
Chambersburg PA
CBHW071857020426
42331CB00010B/2551